Killer Sales Solutions

12 Knock'em Dead Ways to Prepare, Present, and Close the Sale

Tony Navarra

Tony Navarra

ISBN 979-8-9853060-2-6 (hardback)
ISBN 979-8-9853060-0-2 (paperback)
ISBN 979-8-9853060-1-9 (e-book)

Library of Congress Control Number: 2023905585

Illustrated by: Milos Zaric

Edited by: Madeline Parise, Ita de Groot

Book Design by: Tony Navarra

Printed in the United States of America

Published by Tony Navarra

tony@tonynavarra.com

Visit www.tonynavarra.com

Contents

Dedicated to Andy Conn

You believed in me before I believed in myself. Thanks Andy.

Acknowledgements

Writing a book is a collaborative effort. Even though I am the author and the one who put my thoughts and experiences into words, I could not have done it without the help and support of many people. I apologize in advance if I forget to mention anyone who deserves recognition; I have been fortunate to learn from and work with so many amazing people in the fields of sales, persuasion, and motivation.

I would like to express my sincere gratitude to the following people for their contributions to my inspiration and knowledge and other help in creating this book:

To my wife, Toni. You are my rock and my best friend. Thank you for your love and support.

To my children, Mia and Marcus. You are my pride and joy. Thank you for your curiosity and your feedback.

My editors, Madeline Parise and Ita de Groot. You are the ones who made this book possible. Thank you for your guidance and your patience.

I want to thank Marie O'Neal. You were the one who encouraged me to write a book. Thank you for your confidence and your enthusiasm.

Thanks to Michael Robertori and Theresa Deere. You were some of my first sales mentors and inspirations. Thank you for your wisdom and your generosity.

Thanks to Richard Nongard for showing me how to write my first book. You were the one who gave me the tools and the process. Thank you for your expertise and your support.

Thanks to my illustrator, Milos Zaric. You were the one who made my book visually appealing. Thank you for your creativity and your professionalism.

Thanks to all my students, clients, and audiences. You were the ones who challenged me to make things clear and practical. Thank you for your questions and your testimonials.

I want to thank all the people who said "Yes." You were the ones who validated my ideas and my methods. Thank you for your trust and your business.

Finally, I want to thank all the people who said "No" and "Maybe." You were the ones who motivated me to improve and learn more. Thank you for your honesty and your feedback.

Why Read This Book

There is a joke about a Texas rancher. I don't remember the setup, but the punchline has stuck with me for years: "The rancher didn't want to own *all* the land, just the land next to his."

It is the same for me in sales; I don't need to make *every* sale, just the next one. I bet you do too.

If you are a salesperson, you probably know the feeling of wanting to close the next deal. I know I am always looking for an edge in making the sale. After all, sales is a messy business. We never really know why the customer bought something. Sure, they told us some words about why they were buying, but are they true? Do the customers even know themselves why they bought? Wouldn't it be nice to look inside their heads and find out for real?

In this book, you will learn the sales psychology that will help you understand your customers better and influence their decisions. You will discover how to use proven techniques to create a compelling sales environment that your customers can't resist. An environment that demands the customer says, "Yes!"

Chapter One

Introduction

Driving is a dangerous business. It is one of the most dangerous things we engage in— especially when you consider that over 30,000 people died in automobile accidents in the United States in 2021 alone, and many tens of thousands were severely injured during the same period.

Those stats are scary—it's true. But then again, that's what excites me about driving. The stakes are high.

I enjoy sales for the same reason. While I am unlikely to be killed, dismembered, or permanently injured for a poor sales day, there are still consequences that motivate me to go above and beyond.

In sales, the stakes are simply my self-worth, my ability as a man to provide for my family, my sense of agency, and being able to create change in the world. My entire being is at stake. Every. Single. Day. It doesn't matter how many sales I make that day; the next one is where I go all-in to win.

Is this healthy? Probably not. To stake my soul on the whims of another person is probably the least healthy thing a person could do. But oh, how exciting it is to roll those dice.

Like most headstrong people, I am intent on getting my way. I cannot let a simple "No" stand in my way, so I engage in some delusions—or what I refer to as "useful delusions."

I tell myself statements like "It's just a numbers game," or "If I talk to more people, I'm bound to make a sale," or "That rejection doesn't mean anything; water off a duck's back."

Or, more commonly: "I don't care what other people think of me!"

I don't know about you, but I care deeply about what people think about me. I am a total and utter people-pleaser at heart. So I engage in self-delusion to maintain my capacity to act in the world.

The funny thing is that your customers do the same thing. They lie to themselves; they distort their perceptions of the world in order to maintain their beliefs; they change their beliefs, and then they make up a story as to why they always believed that way. They edit their memories to keep their sense of self intact, engaging in the most bizarre mental gymnastics to protect their sense of self.

Once you—the persuader—understand the tangled mess that is all of our realities, reading the minds of others and working with their internal world becomes easy.

We have all attended sales training or read articles on the internet that give us a sales system to follow. There is a multitude of systems out there to choose from, and some will serve you better than others. You can also find advice like "Follow These Seven Steps to Success!" or "Figure Out Your Personality Type!"

More important than the system, though, is understanding the emotions and motivations of the customer. By understanding those, you'll know exactly what to plug into the system to get results.

Let me tell you about my very first sales training. I was nineteen or twenty. I was in college and, like most college students, in need of money. So I answered an ad for telemarketing. They gave me a job right away. That should have been a sign right there, but I was young.

And so I rocked up for my first day on the job. The place was a "boiler room"—I learned the true definition of boiler room that day, as there were probably ten people packed into one stuffy office. We were all on the phone at the same time; dialing, talking, hanging up, dialing, talking, and being hung up on.

Aside from the room, it was a great setup they had going for themselves. They gave everyone a little strip of paper with phone numbers incremented by 3. The last four digits would start with -0000, then -0003, then -0006, and so on and so forth all the way through. We would just dial these numbers methodically.

You didn't know what you were going to get. You didn't know if you would get a home or a business or if you'd get a fax machine or whatever. You just kept dialing.

So there I was, dialing my numbers and getting all kinds of reactions. "How did you get my number?!" "Your call could not be connected." "This is an unlisted number!" "Please leave a message." Everything under the sun.

After a couple of hours of this, I was miserable. I stood up and simply said, "This isn't for me. I'm going to go."

The sales manager, who was probably three or four years older than I was, came over and looked at me. He picked up the phone and slammed it onto the table. In the early eighties, we had these old Bell telephones with push-button dialing—they weighed a ton. It hit with a loud bang, and the bell in the phone rang out clear and long. A hush fell over the room.

"Sit down and keep dialing," he growled.

So I sat down and kept dialing.

That sentence, delivered the way it was, was a sales training and a motivational speech all wrapped up into one.

I don't know how long I worked there—maybe a couple of weeks—but I remember my first sales training to this day.

Sometimes I think that was the best sales training I've ever received. Because it really is true; there will be days, weeks, and months when you just have to keep going and grind it out. Sit down and keep dialing.

In every other aspect, though, my young boss's advice was terrible. He didn't show me how to connect with my customers. He didn't tell me about different customer types. He just implied, *Work this terrible system, and you will either make the sales or you won't.*

With this book, I am offering you my experience with some of the science behind it to improve your sales; when to sit down and keep dialing and when to take a higher-level view of where to place your efforts. You will understand your customer's internal state, and you will take the embers of interest and fan them into the flames of desire.

Working in sales has been my full-time job since 2003. I've engaged in telemarketing, street fairs, in-home demonstrations and sales, and retail sales. I have also been a sales manager. I have hired, trained, motivated, and fired salespeople. And I have fundraised for nonprofits and political advocacy groups.

Even my nonsales jobs had an element of persuasion in them. I used to work for a major railcar leasing company, where I had to get railcars delivered by persuading the person at the other end of the phone to do their job—even if they didn't want to do it.

I worked for the past nine years in a retail shop selling fireplaces and high-end outdoor furniture.

Upon reflection, I can say that sales is a truly diverse and endlessly challenging role. It's also highly rewarding, both financially and emotionally.

Since so much is at stake for me in a selling situation, I want to stack the deck in my favor every time. That gnawing desire to be better has led me to take dozens of classes, read hundreds of books, and practice on the sales floor for thousands of hours. I used to joke that the sales floor was my laboratory—I would take something I learned from Tom Hopkins or Grant Cardone and try it out on the next ten or twenty people I talked to.

I hated to lose a sale.

This book will help you learn to read your customers' minds and understand the emotional motivations behind why they are in conversation with you. Once you understand the emotions—once you understand them in your bones—making the sale is simply taking the next step in the process.

I'm sure you've heard, "You need to develop a relationship with your customer." But what exactly does that mean? You have friends, acquaintances, lovers, partners, and people you wave to each morning. Those could all be considered "relationships," and there's a huge difference between passing acquaintances and lovers. The sales relationship is different again.

The relationship I choose to have with my customers is one of emotional intimacy. Since persuasion is based on emotion, I know of no other way to understand the emotion without feeling it myself. This gives me the strength to have both empathy and tough love when needed. Once people know that you understand and care, they will relax into the conversation, feeling at ease with the sales process.

I guarantee you will get at least one useful thing out of this book. There's going to be some theory, and there's going to be some practice. I have laid out what I know in the best way I can. If you don't learn what to do, you will certainly learn what not to do. I want the investment of your time to be worth it.

As you turn the pages, don't just believe what I say and move on. Instead, say, "Hmm, that's really interesting. Let me give it a try." Then try it. Not just once or twice, but ten or twenty times. Until you become comfortable with the technique, you won't know if it's effective for you or not.

If it works, keep it. Build on it. If not, discard it and try something else.

I will be with you every step of the way through this process. I care about your success. I want you to be successful. I want you to make more money with this than ever. So buckle up. This is going to be a wild ride, and I want you to make it past the finish line.

Chapter Two

The Skills Are Within You (Do You Have What It Takes?)

I was at Fisherman's Wharf in San Francisco some years ago. Since it's a place where many tourists congregate, there are a fair number of street performers gracing the sidewalks every day of the week.

This particular afternoon, there was an old man tap dancing for a small crowd. I stopped and watched. He would start a routine and then flub it up. He did it over and over. You could tell from the sad faces in the crowd that there was sympathy for this man, who perhaps used to be great but had lost his mojo.

My heart went out to the guy. I usually give a street performer ten seconds or so to grab me, but I must have watched this man stumbling and fumbling for at least ten minutes.

I think back on that experience and live in absolute terror of being that guy: the salesman who used to be great but is now doing everything wrong; the one who is pitied by coworkers; the type of pity that turns to anger when their deals are messed up because of his shortcomings.

I want to be the guy who keeps pulling the rabbit out of the hat and beating the odds over and over again, who keeps learning and adapting.

It takes energy and effort to break out of your own limitations and develop new skills. Sure, it does. But what is the alternative? Decay? Decline? Be the next rusty guy or doll tap dancing through the San Francisco streets, merely a shadow of the talent you once flaunted?

***

Reading someone's mind can seem like an implausible fantasy concept to most people, but mind reading is the salesman's trade. Of course, we aren't talking literal mind reading here. There's still, unfortunately, a lot of skepticism about telepathy, but you can come awfully close by using your human powers of observation.

It may surprise you to learn that the skills mind reading requires are the skills you likely already possess. Tapping into those skills, however, is what makes all the difference.

Can people understand you? Do you pronounce words clearly, or is your speech mumbled? Do you use a lot of filler words? Have you learned to communicate with clarity?

Unless you're an athlete or have undergone physical therapy, you've likely never given walking a second thought. But there's a big difference between someone who can only walk ten feet and someone who can hike ten miles.

When I say you already possess the skills to read your customer's mind, that is both peril and promise. Since most of your actions are habitual and automatic, the first step is to become aware of what you are doing.

Becoming a Mind Reader

A few years into my career as a salesperson, I realized I was not looking at my customer. I was looking at the product, the catalogs, even at the floor but not at them. It was difficult for me to look at people. Up to this point, I thought my eye contact was pretty good, but the sudden realization shocked me into action.

I started being more deliberate about looking at people—and, let me tell you, it was hard. It was uncomfortable to look at people that much. I felt emotional, vulnerable even.

Like most things, the more you do them, the more comfortable you become doing them. I improved significantly, but I still had problems looking customers in the eyes. So I kept at it until I'd conquered the fear.

We all have things that we do habitually without realizing it, like picking our nail beds or saying "um" after every few words. Learning to notice and acknowledge these habitual actions is exactly the skill you need in order to effectively mind read for the purpose of sales.

There are two things you are going to have to face in order to read your customer's mind:

1. Be able to reflect on your own actions and see that you have a shortcoming, and

2. Take action to correct that shortcoming.

In my experience, there are many reasons why someone falls short when it comes to reading their customers' minds. A common one is that they rule out emotion entirely from their role as a salesperson, believing that the job is based on rationality, cold facts, and figures. Or perhaps:

- You're afraid you'll misinterpret their emotion;

- You don't want to look like a fool;

- You aren't passionate.

If you identify with any of these sentiments, the question then arises; how do you correct your thinking? It takes a lot of energy to change a habit. But just like I did with making eye contact, you simply need to *try* and stick with it through the discomfort. Read about the emotional aspect of sales. Become knowledgeable about the interpersonal side of your job. Challenge your preconceived notions that sales work is *all about rationality* and that it's *a mask you put on for your customers.*

Once you do this, you're one step closer to seeing your customer as another human being rather than a paycheck or commission. Then you can really start to mind-read.

What does that mean exactly? Does that mean you can peer into their heads and ferret out their deepest fears and desires? Not directly, no, but you can come pretty damn close.

Mind reading has been around since humans evolved, and as we live in groups and rely on our social standing within those groups to survive, it's become a necessity to read each other's minds.

The fact is we are never *not* communicating. Our silences are equally as loud as our words; our eyes talk as quickly as our mouths. In every moment, we are revealing our thoughts. Therefore, mind-reading is simply the act of opening ourselves to the nonverbal cues of unfamiliar people and interpreting them with our innate observational skills.

How do we communicate? Mostly, we do it through our bodies. Body language can show the emotional content of what a person is thinking, from how they hold their shoulders to the number of creases in their forehead. Whether you realize it or not, interpreting body language is integrated into your everyday life.

It's exactly the same story with sales. The only difference between reading your partner's cold shoulder and analyzing the tone of your customer is that one person is familiar, while the other is totally new to you. This creates a mental barrier when trying to interpret their thoughts, but it's by no means an insurmountable one.

Remember that sales are a back-and-forth conversation—one human to another. You're in the same boat. You both communicate in verbal and nonverbal ways, and therefore you can understand one another without necessarily being well-acquainted.

Most prospects are not going to be completely upfront with you at the beginning (if ever) about the problem they are trying to solve. A rehearsed sales talk may come out exactly right, but your emotional melody will be all wrong. This is where your nonverbal reading skills come in handy.

Reading your customers' minds will allow you to speak to them on all levels.

Trying Something New

I remember a piece of advice from Brian Tracy, one of the OG sales trainers. He said you had to try something ten or twenty times before you knew if it was going to work or not. The first few times feel awkward, but hey, just because something feels awkward doesn't mean it doesn't work. It simply means you're not used to doing it.

Modern psychology bears this out. Your brain only wakes up when it's presented with something unusual. And your brain does not like being woken up! It wants everything to be automatic—to be easy.

To be honest, laziness is one of the reasons that I got into sales. I can work part-time. I can work a few hours a week and make a good living doing sales. On the other hand, I like to think of myself as a badass, a go-getter, somebody who grinds away. But those two parts of myself are constantly at odds with each other.

I want to be part of that group of people who just *go, go, go,* and make things happen. But because I'm super lazy, I cut corners. I take risks. I do the things that I'm not supposed to do in all kinds of arenas. And what do you know? Your customers are the same way.

So here's the process: try something new. Try it even if you're scared because what's the worst that can happen?

Feel awkward doing the thing you're trying. As some would say, "Sit in your mud." Allow the discomfort to settle over you like a damp sandy blanket. Feel so transparent in what you're doing that you become paranoid of others calling you out on it.

The discomfort is truly unsettling, but it ends. Next? You get comfortable doing the new thing—so comfortable that you eventually forget you're doing it. The mud will dry up, the sandy blanket will fall away, and you will emerge as someone who has fractionally improved their situation.

But it doesn't stop there because now you've proven to yourself that change is possible. You begin to see room for improvement everywhere in your everyday life—at home, at work, in your hobbies, in your daily routines. This is the cycle of learning you'll follow all your life for a more enriched and vibrant existence. In my case, and for many other salespeople, it's how I learned to mind read.

Find Your Own Style

I am far from the first salesperson to ever write a book. There are plenty of sales systems in existence—systems you can learn like a script for an unfamiliar play; systems you can sign yourself over to and hope for the best.

What I have found is that it's much better to craft your own style. Take a piece of this system and a piece of that one; use the communication strategy from this one and mimic the opening hook from that one.

For example, I love reading books by the big names—Brian Tracy, Grant Cardone, Tommy Hopkins, and the like—as I don't see anything wrong with wanting to learn from world-renowned salespeople, even if they are boomers! But while these are the works of highly successful industry professionals, they tend to outline fairly aggressive sales strategies. And that has just never really been my style.

I have read books on corporate sales like *SPIN Selling*; I have taken the Karrass negotiation class; I have read up on similar strategies for selling to large organizations and long sales cycles, but again, that hasn't really been my style.

My style is more direct; it's more immediate, more collaborative. It's something that I have developed on my own after reading all that I can and testing things out on the sales floor. Over time, I've taken a liking to the styles of Harry Friedman's book *No Thanks, I'm Just Looking* and *The Lost Art of Closing* by Anthony Iannarino, for example. Even *The Challenger Sale* by Dixon and Adamson is more my style.

I like to sit on the side of the customer and help them make a decision for their own benefit. Ideally, that decision includes my product or service, but it doesn't necessarily have to—and that is the style that has always worked for me.

There's hope for people that don't want to have that aggressive approach to selling, the strategy where they must always be closing, always moving, push, push, push. There's hope for people who aren't part of big organizations with intimidating buying groups on the other side of their calls. I know there's hope for those people because *I am one of them.*

Relatively short sales cycles are my sweet spot, but that type of sale isn't usually what the top-selling sales manuals and prolific systems focus on. And that is why, over the past twenty years, I've been developing my own style and doing my own research on how to best approach my markets.

By developing solutions based on experience, my personality, the parts of the systems I admire, and modern research into psychology, I've improved my sales outcomes tenfold. And the people I've worked with as a sales trainer—people who have adopted their own systems—have seen exponential improvements themselves.

So here's what I think: there's hope for us guys and gals in the middle. There's hope for the small business owner and for the retail store that only employs five to ten people. There's hope for the small SaaS shop with just a few salespeople who are tap dancing as fast as they can.

There is hope for you and me.

Chapter Three

Elements of Killer Sales Solutions

"Here, hold this remote," I said to the prospect. "You turn it on by pushing this button."

The command to push the button unsaid, the prospect pushed the button. There was a whoosh as the gas fireplace started up.

I held my hand in front of the glass. "Feel that warmth."

The prospect put his hand in front of the glass and could feel it coming off the fireplace in waves.

"Just imagine how that warmth will feel in your home."

His eyes unfocused a bit, and his shoulders relaxed. All at once, I knew I'd tapped into the right emotions and pressed the right buttons. The sale would be a breeze from here.

I am interested in behavior change. It doesn't matter how the prospect feels; at this point, how they feel will catch up with their actions. I really do not care if they buy a fireplace because they love their family or because they hate their family. I only care about the behavior of buying a fireplace. The emotions will catch up to the actions.

A little harsh, you might say. Perhaps, but we do this all the time. Smile, and your mood will lighten. Slump your shoulders, and your mood will be depressed. Take up more space, and you will be emboldened. Take up less space, and you will become timid.

As Dr. Andrew Huberman of Stanford says, "Mood follows action."

If I can get the prospect to change his behavior, his thoughts, feelings, emotions, and concept of self will follow. By this logic, if I can get the prospect to act like he owns a fireplace, he will begin to believe he is a person who owns a fireplace.

Of course, it isn't quite that simple (if only). Humans are complex creatures; we are not automatons, thank goodness! One of the things I love about my fellow humans, in all their squishy weirdness, is their endless ability to surprise me with their antics.

The Elements of the Killer Sales Solutions

Good things come to those who serve people, and that is what salespeople do. We serve people. We don't serve organizations. We don't serve governments or corporations. We serve people because selling is not purely business to consumer or one business to another. It is human to human. And humans—though they come in a wide variety—share some basic similarities.

These similarities are your entry point into your customer's mind. The similarities will help you change their behavior and their perceptions of your product or service. Once you have influence over the way people perceive your product, you can persuade them to make a commitment, and that's the ticket.

This book is organized into three different sections:

Attractors

Attractors are designed to get people to notice you and then to know, like, and trust you. They are the hook, if you will—the opening actions and behaviors that will either attract or deter your customer.

- **Chapter 4: Physical Environment**

  If you are in a retail environment, this literally means your physical environment. If you are an online concern, it means your website and how it works.

- **Chapter 5: Body Language and Paralanguage**

  We are always communicating even when we do not say a word. That is your body language. Your body is an instrument, learn how to read the music others are sending and how to play the music you are sending.

- **Chapter 6: Elicitation**
  Elicitation allows you to gather information without seeming pushy or making the conversation an interrogation.

- **Chapter 7: Asking Questions**
  Questions direct the mind. Therefore, asking the right questions—questions that cause the customer to think, *Yes, I do need this, don't I?*—are going to help your case and lead you into a sale.

- **Chapter 8: Rhetoric**
  Words are the tools of our trade. Rhetoric is the three-thousand-year-old art that allows you to put yourself and your product or service in the best light. We got democracy from the Greeks; let's take their other goodies, too!

Deepeners

Now that the prospect is paying attention to you, how do you allow them to get to know you in order for them to trust you enough to hand over their hard-earned money? That is where deepeners come in.

- **Chapter 9: Leadership**
  As salespeople, it is our job to lead the prospect through their thought processes until they reach the desired conclusion. You do this by becoming better

at leadership.

- **Chapter 10: Authority**
Authority is the secret sauce, for without it, no one will follow you or listen to what you have to say.

- **Chapter 11: Making and Breaking Trances**
A trance is a state of mind in which your attention is focused on one thing, and everything else is blocked out.

- **Chapter 12: Cognitive Dissonance as a Sales Device**
People love to be consistent and will go to great lengths to make sure they are, from altering their behavior to changing their beliefs.

- **Chapter 13: Meaning-Making**
Humans are Meaning-Making Machines! Things happen and you assign a meaning to them. Help your customers assign the correct meanings to the things that are happening right now and in the very near future.

Activators

Your biggest impediment to making a sale is not the store down the street with lower prices. It is inertia. Most of the prospects I had who did not buy did nothing. Their pain with the status quo wasn't big enough; their desire for something new wasn't strong enough, and they did … nothing.

This is where all the work pays off, or it doesn't.

- **Chapter 14: Categories (or Where to Find the Money!)**
  Most of us have accounting buckets in our heads. This money is for rent; this is for savings; this is for the car payment, and so forth. If you can change the category or the context of the purchase, a whole other bucket of money becomes available.

- **Chapter 15: Post-Close: Persuasion, Manipulation, and Inoculation**
  Keep the sale together, no matter what happens next, even if that means warning your customer about their crazy brother-in-law. (It'll all make sense later on, I promise you.)

- **Chapter 16: A Sale Is Going to Be Made**
  The question is will you sell? Or will you be sold to?

- **Chapter 17: Go Forth and Prosper**

My main hope is that, if nothing else, you understand this: everything you need to be a successful salesperson is already within you.

So that's it, folks. These are skills that you can learn. These are skills that you can use in any sales situation. These are skills that you can use for selling an item or a service, wooing the love of your life, or whatever it is that you want.

So turn the page and begin. Can't you just feel that warmth?

Chapter Four

Physical Environment

All persuasion is self-persuasion. Once I convince myself that something is true, you cannot convince me of anything different. I must do all the work internally to accept what you say; I must follow my own process, make up my own mind, and voluntarily adopt your view of the world as truth. It is only then that I am truly persuaded.

I love my wife. She is the most beautiful woman in the world. She is intelligent and driven. I love her, and nothing you can tell me, show me, or ask me to experience will change that.

Let us flesh out this personal example a little more so that you understand what I mean. Intellectually, I know that my wife is probably not the absolute most beautiful, intelligent, or driven person in the world but this deep and objective understanding is of no consequence to my conscious belief.

All your arguments will break upon the rock of my belief until I persuade myself otherwise.

You are probably thinking, *Excellent. Self-persuasion. How on God's earth do I persuade people to persuade themselves?*

It's an odd question to ask, and it is most certainly an oxymoron. You can't practice mind control on your customers. What you *can* control, however, are the external factors of your sale. The environment, how the product is presented, how you present yourself even—these are guitar strings you can tune perfectly to strum a harmonious chord, all within your grasp and amenable to change.

Controllables

Think about the factors in any sale that you have control over. You can influence the environment to a degree, you can control yourself, and you can present the product favorably. What you do *not* have control over is the initial emotional state of the customer and the process they take themselves through in order to make decisions.

It all starts with the desired end state of the customer. Sometimes that end state is pulling out their wallet and making a purchase, while other times, it will be their committing to the next step of the process. Every end state should have a commitment of some sort, as without a commitment, you are simply deluding yourself.

Speaking of self-delusion—be warned that there is no "Be right back" bus. There will be no sale once a customer says the four dreaded words: "I'll think about it." They will not "Consider it and let you know," nor will they "Visit your website later on." These are fantasies: useless lies that cause you to waste time in a state of hopefulness. Do not get stuck in this trap.

So think carefully: what end state do you want from your customer? When I sold water treatment systems, for example, the desired end state was for my client to purchase the system. When I sold furniture at street fairs, it was for them to purchase a piece of decor right there on the floor. When I sold fireplaces and high-end furniture, I was looking for a commitment to the next step in the process.

But the desired end state is more than just an action. What emotions do you want them to have? Do you want them to feel desire? Love? Greed? Envy? Delight? Eagerness? Once you're clear on that, you can work backward.

When I was selling high-end patio furniture, I wanted my clients to feel eager and a little impatient. I wanted them to ooze with jealousy over their future selves, chewing at the bit in anticipation of showing off their new and luxurious possessions. I wanted them to feel a sense of premature pride over the pieces they were purchasing.

I didn't have to work hard for people to feel impatient. Most of the time, we had to wait a few weeks to get the furniture in the first place. But eagerness and pride in ownership were the feelings I always aimed to encourage.

Control the Environment

Remember that absolutely everything counts. Everything your customers see, hear, touch, and smell will influence their minds, either directing them toward the desired end state or steering them away from it.

I recall a scientific study conducted on people buying wine. They were observed browsing through a selection of French and German wines. If French music was playing in the background, they bought more French wines. If there was German music playing, they bought more German wines.[1] *Everything* matters.

So think about this for a moment. What tools and emotional levers do you have at your disposal? If you have a brick-and-mortar store, it starts with the outside, the parking lot, the curb, and the windows. Is the glass clean? Are your displays well-kept? Or are all the pictures in your windows turning blue from sun exposure? People won't always con-

---

1. Areni, C.S. and Kim, D. (1993) "The Influence of Background Music on Shopping Behavior: Classical Versus Top-Forty Music in a Wine Store" in NA - Advances in Consumer Research Volume 20, eds. Leigh McAlister and Michael L. Rothschild, Provo, UT : Association for Consumer Research, Pages: 336–340.

sciously pick up on your extra efforts, but they'll certainly detect any lack of effort.

If you have a website, does it look clean and modern? Is it responsive and user-friendly on a tablet and phone? Is the navigation easy? Is the server fast?

How do You Present Yourself?

There are two types of authority that are important to this discussion: the way you present yourself and the knowledge you possess to back up that outward appearance.

If you are a doctor who wears a white coat and hangs a stethoscope around your neck, people will assume you have deep knowledge about medicine. Whether they know you or not, they'll likely trust you with their health and life—that is, until they speak to you. Your appearance needs to be supported by sound medical knowledge and a reassuring demeanor.

Initial impressions can elevate you to a position of authority in the mind of your customer. You'll obviously have to back up those initial impressions with ability and knowledge further down the line, but first impressions can go a long way. So let's delve a little deeper into that as we walk through a hypothetical sale.

When the customer enters your store, the way you greet them is imperative. Check your **tone**. Ensure that you are sounding friendly, authoritative, and helpful. Use the inflections of your voice strategically, flicking upward to draw the customer in with questions and inflecting downward to give off a reassuring tone.

It's a balancing act; you want to limit your questions as, at the end of the day, you're the one with the answer to all your customers' problems. At the same time, some customers will rebel if you try to come across as overly authoritative. They will want to argue with you or demonstrate they know more about the product than you do. Some people are just like that. I try not to argue with customers, but some of them love it.

This next point may seem a little fine, but **clothing** does have an impact on your first impression—more than you might expect. What shows authority in your field? A suit and tie? Suspenders and a vest? A silk shirt open to the middle of your chest? A skirt and blouse with a silk bow? A good rule is to dress just a little better than your customers.

Don't mistake me for a clothing connoisseur; I don't know all the finer details about fashion. Back in the Dress for Success days of the eighties and nineties, it was pretty cut and dried. Now, not so much.

Bottom line, you want your clothes to be clean, flattering, and in good condition.

How Do You Move?

What do you think of a person who moves jerkily or erratically? They don't tend to exude authority. People with authority move deliberately and slowly; as Chase Hughes says, you should move as if you are underwater, with no sudden movements and no startling gestures.

Another Chase Hughes suggestion on how to hold yourself is *head over heart, heart over hips.* This will keep you from being scrunched over, allowing you to take a commanding yet humble presence. People who are scrunched over almost scream, "I'm not worthy." Claim your space and make it clear that you're the authority.

Now, let's talk about odors.

Really?

Really.

It's such a small detail, but there's nothing more off-putting than bad breath or untamed sweat patches. Who knows? Maybe those body spray people are onto something.

It's quite simple, really. Be clean and brush your teeth. Pop a mint, even. Wear something fresh. And if you think I'm being superficial here, just take a moment to put yourself in the shoes of the customer. Think back to a time when you tried desperately to battle your way through a conversation only to cut it short because of the other person's unbearable breath.

If a customer can't stop thinking about the smell of onions emanating from your gums, it's unlikely that they'll stick around long enough to buy your dishwasher.

How Do You Relate to the Customer?

Emotions are contagious. As social creatures, we pick up on each other's emotions.

Nobody thinks of themselves as stupid, weak, or ignorant. They are the center of the universe. Their opinions are held because all right-thinking people think that way. Who am I to argue with them? I think the same way. I think I am smarter than the average bear, and I bet you think the same about yourself.

Most drivers think they are better than average. Most teachers think they are better than average. Most parents think they are better than average. This is called the "better than average" bias, and we all suffer from it.

Savvy salespeople and persuaders appeal to this bias. "More discerning people prefer...," "only a few people are able to understand the benefits of..." etc. These statements are all some form of "You are better than most people." Sure, it is flattery, but most people do not see it that way because it appeals to what they believe to be true. As a salesperson, you have to start with where the customer is at in order to lead them to where they want to go.

Uncontrollables

There are so many things we cannot control in life—the weather, the economy, the leadership in our organizations, and the initial emotional state of the customer. Those are things that are simply the way they are. However, we can always mitigate the uncontrollables. We can wear appropriate clothes for the weather, have a nice savings account to handle the economy, and we can meet customers wherever they are when they walk through the door.

You have no idea what emotional state your customer is in when they first engage with you. They could have just had a horrible experience, and you are the next person they encounter. Maybe they take it out on you, maybe they don't, but it will color their entire interaction with you.

Chapter Five

Body Language and Paralanguage

I went to hug the person in front of me. I saw their hesitation, so I slowed down and made my moves more tentative. They became unsure of what to do, so I changed the trajectory of my body and pulled back some. We continued this dance of diminishing expectations until we both stood there awkwardly.

Has this ever happened to you? All without any words being said? That is body language in action.

When most people think about persuasion, they assume it begins when one becomes aware of their target. Somebody walks by you, you see them, introductions are made, and you initiate persuasion with "Let's get to know each other better."

In actual fact, persuasion doesn't start when you become aware of them but rather when *they become aware of you.*

They might not say hello. They may never engage with you or even catch your attention. But from the moment you come into focus in the eye of your customer, your window of persuasion begins.

What this means is that your body language, more than your manners or airs or figures of speech, is what persuades the customer. And since you won't always be aware of the eyes on you, it's important to hold yourself as though you are constantly being perceived.

Body Language as a Device of Persuasion

Your body language says more about who you are than anything else. First and foremost, it indicates your confidence. You are on stage all the time and your performance is especially convincing when the customer thinks they are observing you surreptitiously. The performance is only over when you close up shop for the day.

In that case, then, how do you perfect the art of consistently open and confident body language? There's probably been more written on body language in the last twenty years than there has been in the last two thousand years, so you're in luck.

Joe Navarro, an ex-FBI agent, has written some really great books on body language. I encourage you to seek out his work and learn more about it. In the meantime, what I am going to give you is by no means a comprehensive overview of all body language advice; I am cherry-picking the advice that will yield the most returns.

In other words, if this chapter is 20 percent of all the body language advice out there, it'll give you 80 percent of the possible benefits. I want you to be successful in sales, but I don't want to give you useless jargon.

Let's dive into my personal favorite body language tips:

Smile

Smile, smile, smile, smile. This is a big one. If you've ever been a performer, you'll have had mentors or coaches screeching at you during rehearsals to "Smile! Lift those corners! Raise those eyebrows! I need to see you smiling from all the way back here!"

Luckily for you, smiling in sales is a lot easier than smiling through a musical performance or while playing a flute. Since sales are just everyday interactions with an agenda, you should (hopefully) find it natural to smile back at your customer.

Why smile?

Smiling people are more approachable. This isn't breaking any new ground. They're seen as more friendly, and they make more sales. And if you look into the science and psychology behind why we smile, the reason for this becomes clear.

Humans use the power of reflection in order to connect with one another. When you smile, and someone smiles back at you, they are reflecting and reaffirming the positive interaction you're having. And since we know that (most) smiles are associated with feelings of attraction, enjoyment, and happiness, smiling at someone shows them they can have a positive interaction with you.

When you smile at a customer in sales, you're inviting them to engage in a positive interaction and even reflect the positivity back at you. It's a surefire way to set the stage for a fruitful and constructive conversation.

You may have a resting bitch face. Perhaps life has been difficult, and smiling just doesn't come easily to you. How do you learn how to smile?

One exercise that I learned from Jordan Harbinger is the doorway rule. It's quite simple: every time you walk through a doorway, smile. Give the biggest smile you possibly can. If you smile every time you pass through a doorway, you will learn to smile when you enter a room. You will learn what a smile feels like on the inside, and hopefully, the act will become second nature.

Head Tilt

After smiling, the head tilt is probably my favorite nonverbal device—and what do you know? It really works.

Your neck is one of the most vulnerable parts of your body. Think about it: that cylindrical connection between your head and shoulders contains your trachea, your vagus nerve, your spinal cord, and many important networks traversed by both blood and nerve signals.

When you expose your neck, you risk your life (to put it dramatically). Obviously, you know that nothing is going to happen to your neck while selling refrigerators in an air-conditioned salesroom, but in terms of survival instincts, your neck is something you want to protect at all costs.

All this to say, exposing your neck is an outward display of trust. It demonstrates your ability to be vulnerable around the people in your proximity. And what does this translate into as a salesperson? Going back to the previous section on smiling, showing trust to your customer will prompt them to reflect that trust back onto you.

The head tilt is a very simple move. Don't bend like a garden hose; just a slight tilt to either side will do very well, as you would naturally in a conversation with someone you trust.

Pacing Then Leading

Pacing is another of the greats, and no, I don't mean pacing the perimeter of your sales floor. It makes you look looming—or worse, bored.

What I mean by this is matching steps with someone as you walk alongside them: falling in with their rhythm. It doesn't have to be walking, though; sales doesn't always call for you to walk alongside someone. Instead, pacing in sales can mean matching the customer's tone, mannerisms, rate of speech, and expressions.

Pacing is one of the ways we humans show that we are alike by matching actions. For example: when you see a group of people walking through a busy street together, how do you know they are *together* and not just random people in a bustling crowd?

Typically, they will give very telling signs by pacing. They all laugh in the same way. They echo one another's mannerisms. When one makes a joke, the rest smile and laugh in their direction. They all walk at a similar speed and carry themselves with the same intention.

Another fun game that works well in groups of people is to start matching someone you are not interacting with. Perhaps they are across the room. The only rule is that they can see you. Many times, that person will approach you and engage with you. They do not know why, but they know that they like and trust you. Try it sometime!

After you have matched them for a while and have gained a rapport, you can start to lead. Leading is handy for two purposes:

1. If you want to check to see if you have a rapport. If they follow, they have a rapport with you. If not, engage in more rapport building and then test again.

2. If you want to elicit an emotional state. To get your prospect to adopt a more open body language or a

stance that causes them to feel more optimistic about the future, lead them to that posture.

Eyebrow Flash

The forehead is a very expressive part of the body, and as such, we use it to communicate many of our nonverbal messages and our emotions.

An eyebrow flash is fairly self-explanatory; it's a quick lift of the eyebrows upward. It can be done over a distance, and it is one way we greet each other. This activity is not something that is processed consciously. Like most body language, it is processed subconsciously.

We use our eyebrows and our foreheads to be expressive, but it isn't always in a positive manner. You've heard of people being browbeaten (bullied).

When the eyebrows come down as though they're knitted together, that's a very aggressive signal. The eyebrow flash is the exact opposite. It's a quick *Hey! We're friends. We like each other.*

I like to do this with servers at restaurants because it's a great way to build rapport with them... quickly. In fact, I've flirted with servers and had a lot of fun with them; we were best buddies before the end of lunch.

This is a great way to practice your rapport-building skills because waiters and waitresses are literally being paid to interact with you. They're encouraged to, and you get valuable practice with your nonverbal and verbal abilities, so it's a win-win.

Posture Adoption

Some people have more insight into the inner worlds of other people. They just seem to know what the other person is thinking. Unfortunately, I am not one of those people; I have to study the other person closely in order to mind read.

One of the ways I do this is by adopting the person's posture. If they are sitting upright and open, I sit upright and open: if they are slouched and cramped inward, I try to mimic their position as accurately as possible.

By doing this, I can tune into what my emotions become once they are affected by my posture—and voilà. Now I better understand the other person's state of mind.

For example, you've likely seen depressed people who are worn down and jaded by the tragedies of life. They are hunched over. They have that hangdog expression, and they're pulled into themselves.

That posture has a very specific feeling; it's not a position one adopts if one is feeling confident and content. It's the outward expression of inner turmoil. In order to understand that feeling, you can copy their posture. Now that you have some insight into their internal state, you will be able to better tailor your message for them to understand.

Happy postures are no different. If someone walks toward you in-store, and they are bouncing along, bright and merry, the best step you can take is to echo their posture. This will do two things simultaneously:

- It will allow you to tap into their optimistic and energetic mindset.

- It will show the person that you reciprocate the energy they are bringing into the room.

Body language is a fun thing to practice. It is especially fun to practice on friends and family. You can get into all kinds of trouble by practicing on them; you don't necessarily read their minds, but you certainly get to know their emotional state.

Most emotions are communicated through body language and since sales is an emotional activity, understanding a person's emotions gives you a real advantage when it comes to making the sale.

Paralanguage

Did you know that in conversation, 55 percent of meaning is derived from our body language? Logically, the other 45 percent would come from the actual words we're speaking, right? Wrong.

Paralanguage, which includes pitch, tone, and volume, can account for up to 38 percent of the communication between two people. How we say something can be more important than the words we use.

Paralanguage covers factors like speaking tempo, vocal pitch, and intonation contours. These elements of speech are used to communicate attitudes or other shades of meaning—how you say something, the tone of voice that you use, the rise and fall of your voice; some people call it the "music" of your voice.

However, it's important to note that paralanguage is more specific than whether you shout with aggression or whisper timidly. Do you use flat, declarative sentences? Do you use up-talk, where your voice rises at the end of sentences, which makes them sound like questions? Do you use vocal fry, which gives your voice a gravelly quality? Does your voice have a kind of scratchy quality to it?

Paralanguage is very valuable. Back in the second chapter, I mentioned that one of the challenges to learning how to be an effective salesperson—how to be a *killer* salesperson—is that you assume you already have the skills required to speak effectively.

Fortunately for us, paralanguage is one of those skills that can be learned with very little effort, and the payoff is handsome. Once you're aware that refining your paralanguage is something you should prioritize, it doesn't take much to sharpen your skills.

One of the difficulties of written communication is that it doesn't capture the richness of the human voice. Writers work diligently to capture that difference, and yet most of the time, they fail. It's simply too difficult to convey a character's essence without hearing their voice.

It's one of the reasons email can be such a flat medium and why people get into so many problems working with emails; there's no tone. Granted, emojis make up for some of that; they can fill in a small amount of the lost tone. But there's no denying that the human voice is a rich musical instrument, and it's able to give so much more depth to the meaning of the words that you say.

This is where acting lessons, voice lessons, and articulation lessons come in handy. When you are under the misconception that you already know how to speak because you have been speaking all your life, you don't realize that you haven't developed the ability to speak effectively. It can take a few lessons with experienced professionals in order to wake up to your verbal flaws.

In the meantime, I want to spend the last part of Chapter 5 running through a few take-home points that should be of use to you when selling.

Intonation

First, let's start with the basics of intonation—the rising and falling of your voice. Intonation can be used to communicate a variety of emotions, including excitement, anticipation, doubt, and confusion. When selling, it's important to use the correct intonation in order to match the buyer's emotional state and keep them interested in what you're saying.

This is where we discuss something called *intonation contours*, or the patterns of pitch that we use when speaking. There are three main types:

The **rising contour** is used to show interest or excitement. For example, you might raise your voice at the end of a sentence to show that you're interested in what the other person has to say.

The **falling contour** is used to show that you're finished speaking or to show doubt or confusion. For example, you might lower your voice at the end of a sentence to communicate that you're not sure what the other person is talking about.

The **level contour** is used for most statements and questions. It's neutral and doesn't communicate any emotion.

When selling, it's important to be aware of the intonation contours you're using so that you can match the buyer's emotional state. If they're excited, use a rising contour to show that you share in their excitement. If they're confused, use a falling contour to show that you understand their confusion.

It's similar to the way that you would match someone's physical posture, as I discussed in the previous section on body language. When you're in sync with the buyer, they'll feel more comfortable and will be more likely to trust what you have to say.

Tempo

Are you a student or professor of music? If so, you'll be aware that tempo in a piece of music can completely change the way it's perceived. The same is true in conversation, and it's one of the easiest ways to adjust your paralanguage.

An excellent example of someone who truly mastered the art of speaking tempo was John F. Kennedy. He was known for his incredibly fast speech pace—he set world records, in fact—but he knew exactly how to control the tempo of his words for maximum effect. In his inauguration speech, for example, he purposefully slowed down his speech to create an air of gravitas.

Controlling tempo is a great way to manage the emotions of your listener. A fast-paced sales delivery builds excitement, but only for so long; if you speak quickly all the time, you'll become akin to an irritating fly that your listener can't swat away fast enough. On the other hand, a slow delivery can make you seem like you don't have a clue what you're talking about, or worse, that you're trying to strong-arm them into something.

The key is to read the moment and adjust your tempo to create the desired effect. If you're closing a sale and you see the customer getting antsy, pick up the pace to excite them about what's coming next. Conversely, if you want to build trust and rapport, take things slow and easy.

Pitch and Emphasis

No matter how badly you want that air fryer, you're unlikely to stick around if the salesperson is droning on in a monotone voice (or worse, a high-pitched mosquito whine). Dull, lifeless voices are a surefire way to lose your customer's attention.

Conversely, when you vary your pitch at all the right moments, you engage the listener and keep them hooked. This doesn't mean you need to go full-on stand-up comedian; a simple change in tone can be enough to create variety and interest.

Where you put emphasis on words is also paralanguage. There are a lot of different ways that you can say a sentence, and every new iteration of accented syllables will change its meaning. A simple sentence like, "Mom is driving to the shop," for example, can change its meaning depending on which word is given emphasis.

Emphasis in sales takes a little more intentionality. You want to emphasize the words that will have the most impact on your customer ("money-back guarantee," "free shipping," etc.), and you want to do it in a way that sounds natural and conversational.

If you can get past the embarrassment, a great way to practice emphasis is to record yourself reading a script or talking about your product. Play it back and listen for where you could have put more stress on certain words. If you are open to and can afford it, coaching is a great help too.

Ask yourself this: how quickly do you tune out when someone is speaking to you in a monotone voice? How obvious is it when someone is bored or disinterested in what you're saying? If a friend calls you excitedly and rattles off a fun-filled weekend agenda, how quickly do your excitement levels rise in response?

Avoid the dance of doom! With body language and paralanguage, you have two more channels of communication available to you. Don't do what I did! I showed indecision and timidity to my customer, and it cost me the sale.

Chapter Six

Elicitation

I opened my mouth, tried to push the words out but couldn't, and then closed my mouth. My mind was racing. The ride was going to only last a few minutes, but I was afraid to speak.

I love to chat up my Uber driver. I'd ask about where they were from, how long they'd lived in the area, etc. By the end of each ride, I can rattle off the names of their kids (or give you a rundown of the latest whack-a-doo conspiracy theory).

This time, I had a secret agenda—to find out how much money they made. Not only find out how much they were paid but to do it by asking that question directly.

I was scared. I just knew that they would be able to look through my banter and see with clarity my secret agenda and look at me with disgust at my simple attempt to dig up their secrets. My heart was racing, and my mouth was dry.

I was headed to my hotel from the conference center, where I'd just heard about the ability to discover incredible secrets about a person through normal conversation. *Elicitation.* It sounded like a lot of sneaky spy stuff, and I want to try it out in the "wild."

"I heard you guys had tripled how much you got from Uber," I muttered, using the elicitation technique of a provocative statement.

He muttered a few unintelligible words and fell silent. So that didn't work. I knew he could hear me, and his English was okay, but alas, no answer.

"I've heard that Uber treats its drivers pretty badly. That you guys can hardly take breaks and don't get paid everything you should," I said, using the elicitation technique of criticism.

Bang! The floodgates opened. For the next few minutes, I got an earful of the problems, the bosses, the app programmers, and the passengers. I didn't get to find out how much he was paid on that trip. That would be another trip, but *wow*. It opened my eyes to the power of elicitation, that's for certain.

So what is elicitation? It's simply the ability to get people to talk about themselves and their thoughts and feelings. It's a way of getting people to open up, share what's on their minds, and provide valuable information that you would not ordinarily be able to get.

My Uber driver anecdote is just one example of how elicitation can be used in sales. By simply making statements and being curious about a person, you can learn a lot of valuable information.

In a sales conversation, you want to move with the customer. You do not want to engage in an interrogation, which sounds like you are asking all the questions. Elicitation uses statements that the customer feels compelled to respond to. It perfectly emulates the feeling of a normal conversation.

Before we hop into the techniques, let's examine the word "conversation." In the Latin roots of the word, it means "together to bend or turn." This implies a back-and-forth dance—not a monologue.

Elicitation Techniques

There are many elicitation techniques, but you will find the one or two that work for you. I list just a few that are the most used.

You probably use a lot of these techniques in your everyday and sales conversations. In fact, most of these tactics are just basic back-and-forth conversations. Putting a label on these skills will give you a chance to be more deliberate in your attempts to find out what the customer's needs are and how you can help them.

Bracketing: Provide a high and low estimate to entice a more specific number. "For this type of project, most people have a budget between $3,000 and $7,000."

Response: "We have around $6,000."

This is a great way to qualify someone as well. Once you have bracketed the budget, you know if they have the money and inclination to buy.

Criticism: Criticize the customer or what they are doing right now in the hopes that the person will disclose information during a defense. "Most people just turn up the heater if they get cold." I use this one sparingly and with a light tone. It doesn't really sound like a criticism when I say it. However, a torrent of information will pour out. Suddenly, I know exactly why they want to buy a fireplace, and I can tailor my presentation just for them.

Deliberate False Statements: Say something wrong in the hopes that the person will correct your statement with true information. "Everybody knows that won't work. It will never get off the ground." This technique gets my wife every time. She just cannot wait to correct me!

Dropping a couple of these statements in a conversation can really get the other person talking. "I bet your heating bill is over $1,000 a month." They will either agree with you or disagree. Either way, you have another data point to hone in on in your presentation. If their bill is high, make that a selling point; if their bill is low, don't mention heating bills.

Feigned Ignorance: Pretend to be ignorant of a topic to exploit the person's tendency to educate. "How does this thing work?" This is my favorite technique. A lot of times, I do not even have to pretend I am ignorant! Remember, people like to feel important, and they like to share their knowledge. Make it easy for them.

Flattery: Use praise to coax a person into providing information. "I bet you were the key person in making this decision." It always amazes me how easy this one is. Flattery is one of those things that you think people can see coming from a million miles away. But they don't. I use this one to flavor my conversations, not as the main course.

If I am in the customer's home, I might compliment them on the décor. If they are trying to show off all their "toys," I might compliment them on their prowess.

About 20 percent of the jobs I am involved with are part of a bigger project. So there are a lot of other people involved, including architects and designers. Many times, I will be there with the homeowner along with the architect or designer. I always compliment the design and ask questions about what they are trying to accomplish. This gets me into their thought process and allows me to align my products with their needs.

Good Listener: Listening patiently and validating the customer's feelings (whether positive or negative) is *always* a good sales skill. I almost did not include this as an elicitation technique as it is such a basic human ability. But I realized that it is incredibly rare to find a person who truly listens.

Think about it: most people stumble through their day, interacting with people but simply going through the motions.

These people do not listen; they just act on what they expect to hear.

My uncle-in-law had an uncanny ability to make you think you were the only person in the world worth listening to. It was incredible. It's one of the things his family appreciated most about him.

It is such a gift to be listened to. People who are listened to tend to keep talking and, before you know it, you have their entire life story; the names of their kids and grandkids, where they grew up, their life's work... everything.

There is such a lack of listening right now. All our social media is aimed at broadcasting and consuming, not creating and listening.

Use your awareness to practice active listening because it is truly one of the most important skills you can learn in life and in sales. And who knows? You might get a great business idea, meet the love of your life, or listen someone into a sale.

Shared Interest: Suggest you are like a person based on shared interests, hobbies, or experiences, to build rapport before soliciting information.

The similarity can be as simple as the first letter of your first name. "My daughter-in-law has the same last name as you! Small world."

There is always something you can share with everyone, even if it is something small. Perhaps you have traveled to the same places, or you were born in the same country, or you like the same foods. Your job is to find those similarities and bring them to light.

Disbelief: Indicate disbelief or opposition to prompt a person to offer information in defense of their position. This is very similar to criticism, but instead of going after the person, you are going after what they just said.

"There is *no way* you can do that in less than 30 days and under $100,000!"

I have learned about new construction techniques, ways to navigate the permitting process, and hidden skills people have by using this technique. Just don't sound like you are arguing with them.

I once had a sales manager who thought I was arguing with a customer whenever I challenged something they said. I eventually figured out it was my tone that was coming off as combative. Once I got the tone right, I found that people responded well to my pushback. It got my questions answered, and it elevated me in their eyes to be a partner in the project.

Provocative Statement: Entice the person to direct a question toward you in order to set up the rest of the conversation.

"I could kick myself for not taking that job offer."

Response: "Why didn't you?"

Since the other person is asking, it makes your part in the subsequent conversation more innocuous.

Volunteering Information: Give information in hopes that the person will reciprocate. Sales is often a game of give and take—and you may need to give a little more than the customer at first.

Volunteering information shows the other person that you are simultaneously trusting and trustworthy. It gives them the confidence to offer information in response; some people just don't like taking the first bite, so it's your job to step in.

For example, are you trying to find out the customer's air conditioning needs? Offer information about the climate where you live.

"It's such a humid summer in... " (state your town or city). "I have my aircon on the highest setting, 24/7."

Often the weather is something people quickly grab onto as conversation fodder because it's not too personal or demanding. The customer is likely to respond with similar information... and boom! You suddenly have insight into their air conditioning needs, and the door is open to further back-and-forth conversation.

Word Repetition: Repeat core words or concepts to encourage a person to expand on what he/she has already said. Not only does this demonstrate how attentive you are to what the customer is saying, but it also allows you to emphasize ideas or phrases you want to stick in the customer's mind.

Think about a situation in which your customer continually brings up the high price of fuel (in this case, they are looking for a car with great fuel economy).

You can echo their sentiments back to them by saying, "So you're worried about the high fuel prices right now? That's very understandable. I've got the perfect car for you. It has the best fuel economy across the entire floor."

Instantly, the customer knows that you are tailoring your recommendations to their specific needs and concerns. It shows that you care, and often, it will lead you straight into a sale.

As you go over these techniques, you will recognize that most of them occur already in ordinary conversation. By becoming aware of them, you can now use them deliberately and keep track of the responses. You also become aware of techniques you are not using and can give them a try if they are appropriate for the conversation.

A nice side effect of using these techniques is that you are no longer a "supplicant" or an "interrogator." You are an equal partner. This goes a long way in building the trust you need to make the sale and make your Uber rides a lot more enjoyable.

Chapter Seven

Asking Questions

As the man and woman exited the store, their outlines fading into the dark night, I felt defeat. I had been that close to closing the sale. Then it all unraveled. It was like trying to put water back in a balloon after it popped; nothing I did worked, and it was my own damn fault.

They were a rancher couple who had come into my store in search of a firepit. If I remember correctly, they wanted to pay around $2,000.

I'm a social fellow; I like to talk with my customers and find out their intentions. A lot of the time, they will come in looking for something as part of a much bigger project. They may say that they are looking for outdoor furniture, but they are also looking for an outdoor kitchen, shade structures, firepits, and the like.

Once I found out that the two people in question were ranchers, I remembered there had just been a scandal at a local slaughterhouse, and it had been shut down by the government. I asked the ranchers how that scandal was going to affect them.

It affected them a lot, as it turned out. I got to hear it all: the injustice of shutting down the slaughterhouse, the devastatingly low meat prices, the rising cost of feed. And if that wasn't enough, interest rates were on the rise as well.

Nothing I said or did could stop this spiral of how bad the future was going to be for them. I tried. I talked about the firepit again. I asked them about the options they wanted. *Too late.* The downward spiral had commenced. They walked out into the night empty-handed and angered by their circumstances.

Before you pose a question, ask yourself first, "How does this question advance the sale?" and if it doesn't, don't ask. Keep your eye on the prize: making the right sale to this customer.

Most people use questions as a way of qualifying the customer. Can they afford it? How will it meet their needs? While that is one way to use questions, questions can also be used to direct the mind:

- "What kind of memories are you going to create around this table?"

- "How would you feel if something terrible happened and you didn't do everything you could to stop it?"

- "What do you want to do in your retirement?"

- "What lifestyle do you want your family to have after you die?"

You ask these questions not because you do not know the answers. You ask these questions so the words you want the customer to hear come out of their own mouths.

Let me say that again in a different way. If I told you that $250,000 in life insurance would leave your family destitute after you die, that is a statement that can be argued with. It can be dissected, pondered, and rejected. However, if the customer says that his family will need an income of at least $100,000 a year after he passes, HE is saying those words, not you. When you say it, it is suspect; when they say it, it is the truth.

What Questions to Ask

When it comes to questions, think about what you want to know and where you want to direct the customer's attention. You're not their therapist—they don't need to bare their soul to you in order for you to make a sale. However, you do want to uncover their needs.

The following are some examples of qualifying questions:

- "What are you using it for?" (be specific)

- "Do you have a space for it?"

- "How many people will be using it?"

- "What are your must-haves in a product like this?"

- "What are your dealbreakers?"

- "When do you need it?"

- "What is the budget you're working with?"

These are great examples of product-specific questions, but they aren't always helpful, especially if your customer is hesitant to trust you. A difficult customer calls for more provocative questions that will get them talking.

Some questions that may help with this are:

- "Tell me about a time when you were really happy with your purchase."

- "What's the worst purchase you've ever made?"

- "How do you feel about spending a lot of money on something you won't use very often?"

- "How do you feel about the quality of the products you've been buying lately?"

- "Is there an area of your business that could do with a little improvement?"

The idea is to get the customer thinking and talking. Once they start, they'll most likely continue on their own. It's then that you can interject with questions that will help them see how the product you're selling will solve their problem.

Let's circle back to my initial predicament. Was it wrong of me to ask about the slaughterhouse scandal? It's a fair question, especially considering how it was going to directly impact the ranchers.

In hindsight, it would have been better to wait until after we had talked about the product and they had committed to the purchase. That question derailed the sale, and there was nothing I could do to bring it back.

I'm never going to give a flat rule that says, "Don't you dare ask personal questions!" Sometimes they're unavoidable, and they can even help seal the deal. The key is to use good judgment, and to ask questions that will help you better understand your customer's needs.

Asking for the Sale

Here's a question you may not have considered asking. How would it be if you were to come right out and ask for the sale?

I don't mean that you should beg or grovel. Very few people are going to buy your product if you say "please." What I mean is that there are leading questions you can ask your prospect to move them closer to making a purchase.

One of the most common ways to ask for the sale is to use what's called a "closing question." A closing question is one that gets your prospect thinking about buying your product.

It's not just a question; it's also an invitation for them to take the next step.

Some common closing questions are:

- "What is the next step?"

- "Should we get you started?"

- "When would be the best time to start?"

- "How about we get those forms filled out now?"

- "What do you think?"

- "Is there anything else you need to know?"

These aren't forceful questions; in fact, most customers won't even realize what you are doing. You're just gently guiding them toward the decision to buy.

Can You Ask Too Many Questions?

Yes! It can start to seem like an interrogation after a while. See the chapter on elicitation for other ways to gather the information you need. The key is to make your sales conversation seem as close to a normal conversation as possible.

Ask those questions! Make those statements! Just maybe don't ask questions about the future economic conditions or the latest scandal or the latest sensational crime. Unless it advances the sale, steer clear!

Chapter Eight

Rhetoric

I used to think of our ancestors as being less than intelligent. After all, they didn't have television or the radio. If you go back far enough, they didn't even have widespread access to literature. And what about ancient civilizations? How smart could you be if blood sacrifices and fighting to the death were regular occurrences?

As I have learned more about them, however, I realized that humans in the past were not dumb. Sure, there was more disease and hunger, and they didn't live as long, but they were just as intelligent and driven as we are. And since they were not watching reruns of *Gilligan's Island*, they had more time for conversation and arguing with each other.

The Akkadians of Mesopotamia first wrote down their system of argumentation over 5,000 years ago. The Greeks were good at this, too, and wrote their own comprehensive system around 3,000 years ago. Theirs is called the Art of Rhetoric, and it remains with us to this day. (Thank you, scribes of Andalusia and monks of the Middle Ages!)

Before you say, "Ugh! Who wants to hear about ancient history?" Think about this: thousands of years ago, empires rose or fell on the strength of their arguments. The nobility trained their children in the art of argumentation. Wars may have been fought on the field of battle, but they were won or lost in the hearts and minds of the people involved.

And that's what rhetoric is; the ability to win people over to your point of view. It doesn't matter if you're selling a product, a service, or an idea—if you can make your case convincingly, you will be successful.

My definition of rhetoric is a little different from most. It is the art of keeping the rational mind busy long enough for the emotions to become engaged. The emotions, once engaged, will drown out the voice of reason.

Modern neuroscience has shown that the emotions make a decision, and the rational mind makes up reasons why it made that decision. While you or I might talk about how "rational" our decisions are, the true decision was made when an emotion became crystal clear in our being. It's all window dressing after that.

Rhetoric is a powerful tool, and it can be used for good or for ill. The best salespeople are those who can use rhetoric to appeal to their customers' emotions without making them feel like they are being manipulated.

I have a couple of book recommendations when it comes to learning rhetoric. Check out the Resources Chapter for them. This chapter is an introduction to some of the concepts you can use today in a sales conversation, but truly, you could spend years learning this topic.

What Is Your Goal?

In a sales conversation, you always have a goal. Always. Every word, every gesture, everything in the environment is dedicated to one thing. What is that thing? Your ultimate goal is to make a sale, but that is not necessarily your goal in a particular situation or at a particular time.

Everything you say has to do one of three things in service of your goals: stimulate the customer's emotions, change the customer's opinion, or get the customer to act. The list is in order of difficulty.

The emotions I most want to stimulate are desire, curiosity, and mild fear. Desire gives them a goal to move toward, curiosity keeps them eagerly moving ahead, and fear nips at their heels.

Take the position of a used car dealer, for instance. Your objective is to arouse the customer's emotions so they will desire to purchase the vehicle. You may use language like, "This car has received a lot of love. Look at how spotless the inside and outside are. It's clear from the condition that the prior owner took good care of it."

The change in opinion goal is a little more difficult. You have to get inside the customer's head and understand what they are thinking, then change their thinking. This is where you use facts and logic to support your position. For example, if you are selling a car and the customer says, "I don't like how small it is," you could use logic to show them that a smaller car will save them money on gas and insurance.

The last goal—getting the customer to take action—is all about giving them a clear path to follow. For example, if you are selling a car and the customer says, "I don't have the money to buy it right now," you could say, "That's no problem. We have financing available. Just fill out this application, and we can get you in the car today."

That being said, remember that your customer *always* has a preset opinion about your product or service. Your goal, then, is to alter their opinion. If their opinion is in favor of the product or service, do nothing to change it. In fact, you can talk yourself out of a sale if you work on their opinion too much. Less is more here.

If their opinion is "Maybe" or "No," do not go directly against it. I try to increase the options they are aware of to make my offering more appealing.

For example, perhaps they want to use their backyard for more entertaining, but they think it would be too expensive to include an outdoor kitchen. I would start questioning around this. How many people do they expect to have over?

Where do they want them to sit? Do they want a firepit or some other central gathering point?

Then we would get around to the preparation and serving of food. Where is that going to take place? How many steps are there to where the entertainment will take place? How can we make that easier for the host or hostess (aka, your customer) so they can enjoy the party too?

After a while, some sort of outdoor cabinetry starts to make sense as part of their overall plan and their happiness. Game, set, and match!

Intermediate Goals

Sometimes—most of the time, even—your ultimate goal isn't going to be attainable from the get-go. You need to break it down into smaller goals. This is what we call "intermediate goals," and they're all about getting the customer closer to doing what you want them to do.

Here are some more examples of intermediate goals:

- Progress to the next stage of the sales process.

- Get an email or phone number.

- Get the prospect to listen to you.

- Get the prospect on the phone.

- Develop a relationship with a key contact.

- Gain market information from the prospect.

One of the most basic intermediate goals is getting the customer's attention. Once you have it, you have to keep it. You can do this by being interesting, relevant, and helpful.

Another intermediate goal is establishing common ground with the customer. You want them to know that you're not just some talking head trying to sell them something—you're a person they can relate to. You can do this by sharing personal stories and using language they understand.

These intermediate goals don't create a sale by themselves, but they're necessary precursors. Once you've got the customer's attention and they feel like you're someone they can trust, you can start making your pitch.

I sometimes think about my intermediate goals as military retreat tactics; it feels like defeat at first, but I am merely accepting a small setback or delay in order to make progress. "Can't get the sale today? Okay, I'll have them accept a written quote."

This is why having a system is so important; you know what the next step is going to be, so there's no moment of panic when the sale doesn't immediately land.

You can also think of intermediate goals the other way around. For example, almost every fireplace sale I made required a site visit. So instead of selling the product, I focused on selling the site visit instead.

This was an easier sale, and it got me another interaction with the customer. I had to be careful, though. If all I did was sell the site visit, I would not have laid a strong enough foundation to make the sale in the home. I needed to make sure that the customer would be present. I had to be prepared with questions and incentives.

Who Is Your Audience?

Imagine that you are in the process of pitching a sale. You have one person in front of you; they are interested in your product, they are qualified, and you are giving your sales presentation with their needs in mind.

Here's a trick question: who is your audience? Obviously, the person in front of you, right? Ah! The tricky element to remember is that there may be a lot of other people involved.

For example, what if your customer is in a relationship? They may have a spouse or significant other that they need to discuss the purchase with. Alternatively, they may have a best friend they want to convince or impress.

Let's widen the scope a little further. What if the audience is your boss? Perhaps your numbers are down, and the boss is watching your sales to see where they can "help."

Another possibility—one that pops up more often than you might think—is that your audience is the customer's critical inner voice. Maybe they have the voice of their mother or father stuck in their head, telling them what to do. It could be the case that the customer is a perfectionist, and their inner critic is warning them *You'd better make the right choice!*

The point is you might be talking to multiple customers at once regardless of whether they are present and tangible in front of you. Being aware of these secondary customers can make all the difference in the success of your pitch.

Try to find out the other players in the decision-making process. One of my favorite questions is, "Besides yourself, who else will be involved in this decision?" You won't always get all the information you need, but it's a good step in the right direction.

Rhetoric Terms

Now the moment you've been waiting for—it's time for some Greek words. (Don't worry, you've probably seen them before.)

These are the rhetorical principles we've adopted from our ancestors, and to this day, they stand incredibly strong as argumentative strategies. Let's take a closer look.

Many consider Aristotle as the father of rhetoric because he defined three modes of persuasion: ethos, logos, and pathos. Ethos is about establishing credibility; logos is about using reason and evidence to make an argument, and pathos is about appealing to the emotions.

Logos: Argument by Logic

Logos is an appeal to rationality. While some emotionally driven arguments are strong enough to stand on their own, a logos-based argument is stronger and more convincing. It's the difference between saying, "I think you should buy this product because I like it, and I think you will too," and "I think you should buy this product because it has features X, Y, and Z that will benefit you."

The use of logos in sales is all about providing evidence for your argument. This could be in the form of statistics, customer reviews, expert opinions, or any other type of factual information. When making a purchase decision, people want to know that they are making a wise choice. Providing evidence for your argument helps to build trust and credibility with potential customers.

Pathos: Argument by Emotion

Have you ever encountered animal welfare activists who hold screens with photos of abused animals as they protest at your local butcher's shop? The aim of these activists is to evoke an emotional response in order to convince you to change your behavior. This is an example of pathos or argument by emotion.

Pathos is a device used to tug at the heartstrings of an audience in order to persuade them to take a certain course of action. In a sales context, pathos can be used to create a sense of urgency or highlight the negative consequences of not buying a product or service.

For example, imagine that you are selling insurance. You could use pathos to emphasize the potential financial hardship that could be caused if something were to happen and the customer did not have insurance. You could also highlight the peace of mind that comes with knowing that you are insured in the event of a disaster.

Ethos: Argument by Character

Imagine for a moment that you are trying to decide whether to buy a new car. First, you ask your family for recommendations. Your dad chimes in with, "I've always been happy with my Ford."

Your little sister pipes up, "I don't know anything about cars, but I think you should get a pink one!"

Armed with the opinions of your loved ones, you begin to do some research on your own.

Soon enough, you find yourself at a car dealership. The salesman there greets you warmly and asks what he can help you with. Not only is he friendly but he's also equipped with knowledge about the exact model of car you're interested in. He tells you about the features, how it drives, and even shows you that his personal car is the same model.

After listening to the salesman and doing some more research on your own, you decide to buy the car. What persuaded you? The salesman's ethos—his character and reputation.

He came across as someone who knew what he was talking about, so you were more likely to believe him. (A pink car would have been fun, but your sister doesn't stack up to a professional salesman!)

Ethos is an incredibly powerful tool for salespeople. Think about the celebrity-endorsed skincare products you see on TV and the celebs absolutely glowing with perfect poreless skin. Think about the athletes who promote energy drinks or the actors who shill for car companies. They all have one thing in common: a (seemingly) trustworthy ethos.

When you see someone you trust promoting a product, it's much easier to be swayed into buying it. After all, if they believe in it, why shouldn't you?

In your own sales interactions, try to create a persona of authority and knowledge. Be sure to know your product inside and out, and be able to answer any questions your customers may have.

When you come across as someone people can trust, you'll be well on your way to closing the sale.

Time in Speech

When delivering a sales pitch, rhetoric isn't just applicable to the types of arguments you present. It's also about the tense you use when speaking. Believe it or not, the time frame you put your words in can have a significant impact on how persuasive they are.

Consider this sentence: "I could have saved you a lot of money if you'd contacted me sooner." The use of the past tense here emphasizes that whatever action the listener didn't take has already passed. This may make them feel regretful or like they missed out on an opportunity.

Now compare that to this sentence: "I can save you a lot of money if you contact me soon." The use of the present tense, in this case, makes it sound like saving money is still an option which may be more persuasive to the listener.

Of course, there are exceptions to this rule. Sometimes you may want to use the past tense to emphasize how serious an issue is or to make your argument sound more certain. But in general, using the present tense is typically more persuasive when trying to sell something.

Let's take a closer look at the specifics:

Forensic Rhetoric

When we use the past tense in our speech, it is usually interpreted as blame. For example, if I say, "Why haven't you got an insurance policy yet?" the implication is that you should have gotten one by now. This type of rhetoric is often called "forensic."

Forensic rhetoric originates from the Latin word "forensis," meaning "forum." In ancient Rome, this was the name given to the public square where legal proceedings were held. Lawyers would use forensic rhetoric in an attempt to win cases by shaming their opponents.

When used in a sales context, forensic rhetoric can be very effective in convincing people to take action. For example, you could use it to make the listener feel like they're missing out on an opportunity if they don't buy your product. It highlights the benefits of taking action *now* rather than *later*.

Demonstrative Rhetoric

In sales—or arguments in general—an excellent tactic is to separate the good from the bad. You can do this by using what's called "demonstrative rhetoric," which uses present-tense speech to highlight the benefits of a product or idea while putting the drawbacks in the past.

Imagine you're selling a new piece of software. You could say something like, "This software is amazing! It can do things that no other software can." By emphasizing the positive features of the product in the present, you're more likely to persuade the listener to buy it.

However, you should also be prepared to address any potential drawbacks of the product. So if someone asks about compatibility issues with other software, you could say, "We've tested it extensively and haven't had any problems so far." By putting the negative information in the past, you make it sound like less of a concern.

Deliberative Rhetoric

We've talked about rhetoric from the past and present, so what's left? The future, of course. Deliberative rhetoric is all about using persuasive language to get someone to take an action in the future.

This type of rhetoric is often used by salespeople when trying to get a customer to sign a contract or agree to a purchase. It's also used in political speeches when the speaker is trying to get the audience to vote for them or support a particular policy.

So how does it work? In general, deliberative rhetoric tries to appeal to the listener's sense of reason and logic. The speaker will make an argument about why taking a certain action is the best choice for both parties involved.

They may also try to evoke emotions in the listener, such as fear or hope. By doing so, they can influence how the listener thinks about the situation and make them more likely to take the desired action.

The Sapir-Whorf Hypothesis

Have you ever heard of this theory? It's generally referred to as "linguistic relativity," and I find it absolutely fascinating. The hypothesis, proposed by Edward Sapir and developed further by Benjamin Lee Whorf, essentially states that the language we speak both shapes and limits the way we perceive reality.

It's an interesting notion, and although it's faced plenty of rebuttals over the past century, I think there's still a lot of merit to it. Let's take a look at an example.

In the Western world, our perception of time is incredibly linear. We see our years stretched out before us like a road, with each step taking us closer to the end. But other cultures perceive time quite differently. The Hopi, an indigenous tribe from North America, see time as a cycle. There's no beginning and no end—just an eternal present.

If you were to ask a Hopi person about time, they would give you a very different answer than if you asked a Californian. And that's because the Hopi language doesn't have words for "past" and "future." The only time that exists is the present.

The Sapir-Whorf hypothesis would argue that this difference in perception is due to the Hopi language's lack of words for "past" and "future." Without those words, the Hopi people are supposedly unable to conceive of time in a linear way.

I think this is a great example of how our language can shape our reality. And, while words do not necessarily limit or constrain what you can think about, they do guide the mind. If you say water is tepid, for example, that means something different from if you said it was lukewarm. There is a different connotation between those two words. Your words will shape your customer's experience; choose them carefully.

Linguistics in Sales

As sales professionals, we're constantly trying to persuade our prospects to buy our product or service. And to do that, we need to understand our prospects' worldviews. We need to understand the way they see the world and the language they use to describe it.

If we can do that, we can start to speak their language. We can start to think like them and see things from their perspective. And that's essential if we want to persuade them to buy from us.

So how can we go about doing that? It's not always easy, but there are a few things you can do.

First, start with the product or service you are selling. What are its benefits? How does it solve your prospect's problem? Firepits, for instance, provide heating, ambiance, and cooking capabilities for outdoor spaces. You want your words to point to the emotional or physical benefit of your product or service.

Tables provide an eating and living space. Books provide knowledge and stories. Insurance policies provide safety and security. When you can articulate the benefits of your product or service in a way that resonates with your prospect, you're well on your way to persuasion.

No matter how you approach this, you want all your words to point to one thing—the customer needs to own the product or service.

Thought-Terminating Clichés

In the fifties, there was an American psychiatrist by the name of Robert Jay Lifton who studied the use of thought-terminating clichés. It's essentially a way of shutting down debate or critical thinking by using a phrase that's so overused it's become meaningless.

When you were younger, did your parents ever try to assert their authority by simply saying, "Because I said so"? In cases like that, "Because I said so" is a thought-terminating cliché. It doesn't actually explain anything or provide any justification for the opinion being expressed. It just shuts down further discussion.

Or perhaps you've had awful circumstances explained away by someone appealing to God's "mysterious ways." I'm willing to bet that this didn't make you feel any better.

Thought-terminating clichés can be incredibly damaging because they prevent people from thinking critically and challenging the status quo. But they're also incredibly common in our society. We hear them all the time in politics, in the media, and in our personal lives.

In sales, we hear a lot of thought-terminating clichés used to try and close a deal. For example, "It's a no-brainer" or "This is a great opportunity." These phrases may sound persuasive, but they don't actually mean anything. They're simply used to make the decision appear easier than it is.

Where possible, I implore you to avoid thought-terminating clichés in your own sales conversations. If you're looking for a way to close the deal, try explaining the benefits of the product or service in detail. Show your prospect that you've put thought into this decision and that you're not just trying to shut them down.

Substance-less words are tempting, I know, but they won't get you very far in the world of sales.

The Power of Words

Let's talk about it. Why are our words so important when it comes to sales? What's the impact of words on our ability to seal a deal?

Words in and of themselves are just symbols. They have no inherent power. It's the meaning we give them that matters.

Think about witchcraft for a moment (it's relevant, trust me). Why do you think witches referred to their curses as spells? Take a guess.

In the days of the Spanish Inquisition, when witches were being exposed left, right, and center, a reality of the time was that most people did not know how to spell.

In *Beauty and the Beast*, when Belle was scolded for reading stories to children in the village, it was because the ability to spell gave people power.

Therefore, the word "spell" was associated with something that could make an impact, something with power; hence witches used the word to refer to their curses.

Here's another example. In Judaism, the Hebrew word for "God" is never said out loud and never spelled out in full. This is because the actual word is afforded so much respect and reverence that it's seen as too holy, too powerful, to speak aloud.

Then, of course, there are contracts. This is an example you're more likely to be familiar with. How often have you signed an insurance contract only to find out later that certain words and phrases in the contract were actually defined in a way that was advantageous to the company?

The use of specific language in a contract can often mean the difference between someone winning or losing a case. Why? Because the words we choose carry weight. They have power.

Word Choices in Sales

When it comes to sales, the words you use can mean the difference between a customer buying or going elsewhere.

It's very important that you choose the words most likely to paint your product or service in the most favorable light. Think of the old "glass half full/glass half empty" analogy. One phrase has a negative connotation, while the other has a positive one.

Here's how I suggest you go about choosing your words. Start with your intention. What emotion do you want your customer to feel in response to the words coming out of your mouth? Then figure out the words that will best create that emotion. If you want them to feel excited, use words that convey excitement. If you want them to feel confident, use words that convey confidence.

And remember, it's not just about what you say, it's also about how you say it. This chapter plays along perfectly with the previous one. Combine the power of rhetoric, body language, and paralanguage, and you have a recipe for success, and you will be as smart as our ancestors.

Chapter Nine

Leadership

Once upon a time, in a former life, I was a bohemian. I lived in San Francisco, hung out at Café La Boheme at 24th and Mission Streets, smoked American Spirit cigarettes, drank coffee, and read important books.

I was sitting at a table one day (predictably) reading a book on leadership when a friend of mine sat down as well. His name was Bernie Katz.

Bernie was an economics professor who loved to travel to different countries and teach. He had taught at a Chinese university in the early eighties, had recently returned from teaching in Japan, and was currently teaching at a school in San Francisco.

Bernie and I got along well; we always had the best conversations together. We would debate the issues of the day as well as the meaning and means of a good life. He always had pithy advice for me. This day was no different.

"You want to be a leader?" Bernie asked.

"Sure," I replied. "All the articles I've read and people I've listened to say that you need to be a leader. I'm trying to figure out what that means."

"The secret to being a leader is to make decisions," said Bernie. "Most people are afraid to make decisions, and they will readily give over leadership to anyone who will make decisions for them."

I didn't know it at the time, but that was one of the most important pieces of advice I have ever received. It was so much simpler than any advice a leadership guru could offer, too.

As a salesperson, you are the leader in the seller/customer dynamic. I know many salespeople who do not feel this way; instead, they feel like supplicants. *Please, Mister Customer, give me your money!* ... groveling their way to a measly, wrangled commission. That's no way to live.

As a salesperson, you need to take the lead and make some decisions on the customer's behalf. You know your product. You know what will work and what will not, what options they will need, and the *must-haves* versus the *nice-to-haves*. You need to decide what the customer needs to own and then take that customer on a voyage of discovery so that they come to the same conclusion.

The only decision the customer can make is *Yes* or *No*, regardless of whether they make it with you or with someone else. To paraphrase Yoda, "Maybe there is not. Only yes or no."

After you ask questions and diagnose the problem, then you can come up with the solution. Once you know the solution, the real work of a salesperson begins—taking the customer by the hand and walking them through the steps so that they come to the conclusion you want them to have.

Here's your process:

1. Understand the problem.

2. Come up with a prescription or a solution.

3. Work backward from the solution to the current state.

4. Walk the customer through those steps.

Let's say a customer wants to buy outdoor furniture so that they can entertain in their backyard.

"How many people will be there?"

"Will they be eating?"

"What are the sun/shade preferences?"

"How will we keep them warm in the evening?"

By asking a few choice questions, you discover they will want to serve food to their guests, but the inside kitchen is far away, and they don't think they can afford an outdoor kitchen.

Now you need to make some decisions. Do you ignore the whole issue and just go with what they came in with? Do you ignore their complaint that it is too expensive and build a kitchen into your presentation?

There is no right or wrong answer here. I have done both with mixed results. I have gone with what the customer told me and then later had them angrily tell me, "Why didn't you say something?" I have also talked the customer out of a sale because there were too many things to think about or it was out of their budget.

If you don't know which way to go, simply give them all of the options. At the very least, it will help you build trust and rapport with the customer while you open their eyes to additional possibilities.

For the sake of our example, let's say you decide that the customer will benefit from an outdoor kitchen, and you have a pretty good idea of what the kitchen needs to be made up of.

Take another mental step in the construction of the kitchen and start to build a list of items and their associated benefits. For example, they probably should have a grill. How would a grill benefit them? If they were older, it would save all that walking back and forth into the house—easier on the knees that way. If they are younger, it could be the ability to be outside with their kids instead of being stuck in the house for half the party. The benefits would depend on the customer.

Now you're ready. You can start the presentation and lead them through the process so they can come up with the right conclusion. The customer can always say yes or no, but remember, if they didn't want your input, they would have gone straight to the cash register with the first product they saw.

Taking Customers through the Process

What does that mean, exactly? There are two ways you can do it. You can pull them through the process, or you can push them through the process. Pushing someone through is exactly that—it's pushy and tends to have less buy-in from the customer.

The easiest way to push someone through the process is to use a lot of tie-downs. "Wouldn't you agree that keeping an eye on your children in the backyard is important?" "Don't you need a larger table to seat all your guests?"

I try to use this only when the customer is having a hard time coming up with the right answer on their own.

Pulling someone through the process involves the use of a lot of questions.

"How good are you at navigating stairs while carrying heavy plates of food?"

"How much supervision do the kids need while they are in the backyard?"

You want to create an aha moment for the customer where it all clicks into place, and they know with crystal clarity what the next step is. The key is for them to come up with it on their own.

You could, of course, just tell them the conclusion, but then it can be argued with, questioned, and discounted. If the customer says it, then it is the truth—to be accepted without further debate.

Questions Prompt the Process Along

I like to ask questions that will guide the customer's thought process. Refer back to the chapter on asking questions for more details. Remember that the content and tone of your questions will direct the customer's attention. You want the attentional spotlight firmly on the path you have laid out for them.

"How will you use the space?"

"What challenges do you expect in reaching your goal?" or

"Imagine the memories that you will create around this space with your family."

These types of questions do a few things:

- They put the customer in a position of ownership.

- They get the customer to imagine how they will use the product.

- If your customer is like most people, their imagination will gloss over the details and focus on the big picture.

That big picture can either be positive or negative, which is where the tone of the questions really comes in. You want the tone of the questions to be negative if it is something you do not want them to be doing and positive for the things you want them to do.

And remember, you need to ask the right type of question, too. Closed-ended questions can only really be answered with a simple "Yes" or "No." If you have watched any courtroom drama, you have seen the witness trying to explain what they meant and the attorney saying, "Just answer yes or no." Finally, the witness has to answer.

It can feel that way sometimes to your customer, which is why you need to use the push method sparingly. Only use it when their imagination has failed them at some point, and you have to get them to the next step.

The use of the pull method is more fun and enjoyable, even if it takes a little longer. Your good friends *What, Why, When, Where,* and *How* are at your service here. Get the customer to expand. Get them to go on and on and on. "Tell me more" is a great prompt. A few "ahs" and "uh-huhs" help too. Keep the floodgates open.

Only intervene if the direction takes a turn somewhere you do not want to go. You are in control here. Ultimately, this is your conversation—just don't make it seem like you are the one in control.

Be Prepared

In reality, there are only a few things that are going to come up in a sales conversation, so get really good at those few things.

You know what your customer is going to ask, so write down the best answers and practice them. You know what your customer's objections are going to be, so kill the objections before the customer even verbalizes them. You know what questions are going to direct their mind, so write those out and practice and refine them.

It used to baffle and frustrate me when the customer would ask for a discount, and I didn't have an answer. It was like I had been asked this for the very first time; it always caught me flat-footed. It was years before I actually scripted out a few things so that I could have some coherent thoughts together when I got that zinger at the end.

I boggle at the amount of money I gave away, the number of sales I lost, and the hours I spent explaining away a heinously low net income to my sales manager or business owner. Take it from me and save yourself the pain. After a little while, you will know 80 percent of what is going to happen in the sales conversation.

Shift Your Perspective

Look at the whole sales transaction from the buyer's perspective. They have limited time, money, and attention. They don't have all the time in the world to negotiate with you. They do not have an unlimited budget, and they cannot give this project all their attention.

If they see you as their trusted partner, then a lot of things will fall into place for you. The customer wants to feel good about their purchase. They want to get this over with and sleep well at night. Sure, they can get it cheaper down the street, but then they will stay up all night with worry that something is going to go wrong or that they will get stuck with something much bigger than they wanted in the first place.

Being able to work with a trusted representative beside them no matter what happens is worth a lot to them. After a while, the high cost will fade from their minds, and they will simply enjoy the final result. It is like childbirth—the pain of labor is forgotten, and all the wonderful memories of motherhood are formed. Take the sage advice of my friend Bernie and make a decision for them. If you don't, nothing will happen.

Chapter Ten

Authority

I strode through the loading bay. There was a bustle of activity around me as people unloaded their trucks and were moving things further into the cavernous building. The *beep, beep, beep* of forklifts reverberated around me.

A group of security guards were checking that people had vendor badges and were allowed into the building. I did not have a vendor badge on display. Instead, I briefly joined a group going through the checkpoint but continued my pace of walking forward.

I looked at one of the guards, nodded slightly, and gave her a small smile. She looked at me and waved me through. The victory dance could wait till later.

In this case, I was supposed to be there at the loading bay, but my badge was tucked away in my back pocket. By rights, every security guard should have asked me to display it. So what happened?

Quite simply, I looked like I belonged. I acted like I belonged. Other people treated me like I belonged. Therefore, I belonged, and no one questioned it.

I don't know about you, but for me, I enjoy treating life as a big game of *What can I get away with?* I don't play it to hurt anyone: just to make observations about people and life and to learn.

This particular game was to see how far I could get into a venue without displaying any documentation. Some places were like Fort Knox. There was a place in Sacramento where I couldn't turn around, and someone was eyeing my badge. Some places, I just strolled on in and spent hours without donning my badge.

The lesson I learned was an interesting one and a valuable asset to my skills as a salesman.

We're All Sheeple

We are social creatures. We look to each other for cues as to how we should behave in an environment. If something happens and nobody looks concerned, we assume that there is nothing to be concerned about.

There was a scientific study done in the sixties by Dr. Stanley Milgram (more about him later) and two other researchers where they had people stand on a busy street corner and look at something in the sky. The question was, "Will other people stop and look?"

They had groups of one to four confederates look up. The more confederates there were involved in the study, the more people stopped and looked up at the sky. Even more people joined the fray when the confederates were well-dressed.

It is easy to look at that and think *Ugh, what a bunch of sheeple!* Sorry to burst your bubble, but in reality, you do the same thing all the time—and that's not a bad thing. If you see a group of people screaming and running in one direction, you might want to do the same to get away from the tiger.

Stopping on a street corner and looking up is one thing, but what if someone needs help? Studies have shown that people will step over people moaning for help on the street, especially if they are dressed like they are homeless. However, if the person moaning on the street is dressed well, people will stop and help.

The moral of the story is that if you are going to get in trouble, dress well first! Only joking, of course. There's no real moral here. Just an observation that we are indeed social creatures, and we derive meaning from our cultural and environmental cues.

Authority and Atrocity

After WWII, there was a lot of interest in authority and obedience to authority. The atrocities of the Nazis shocked the world, and the refrain of "I was just following orders!" came from the lips of many war criminals. So the question was fresh in people's minds when psychologists and sociologists started doing these experiments to test the power of authority.

In the fifties, Dr. Solomon Asch conducted a now-famous study called the "line conformity study." There would be a group seated around a table looking at a set of lines projected on the wall. There was only one participant, and the rest were confederates. A confederate is a person who is part of the experiment, not the subject of the experiment.

The question for the group was, "Which line is longer?" Then each person, in turn, would give their answer out loud. The answer was always obvious—there were no "pretty close" answers. After a few rounds of the confederates giving correct answers, they then gave a blatantly false answer.

Imagine you're sitting at a table; each person has given an obviously wrong answer, and now it's your turn. What do you do? If you're like most people, you, too, will give a false answer. You will distort your own senses in order to conform to the group. After all, the majority rules. Aren't they more likely to be right?

This study has been run thousands of times with different variations. What happens when the participant is the first person to give an answer? Last person? Middle of the pack? What if everyone writes their answers down secretly? The findings are consistent; if you are toward the back of the line and everyone gives their answers out loud, you will probably fall in line (pun intended!).

One interesting variation of this experiment involved a group of people sitting in a room filling out a survey. Again, there was only one real participant, and the rest were confederates. They could hear a smoke alarm going off in another room, and smoke began to waft under one of the doors.

All the confederates continued nonchalantly filling out the survey as if nothing was happening. Even though each participant was usually concerned, they rarely took action to leave the room, even as the smoke got thicker. It only takes a few minutes of smoke inhalation to kill you, and they would have all died if there had actually been a fire.

Conformity and obedience to authority couldn't just kill you; it could cause you to kill as well. Dr. Stanley Milgram didn't stop at having people stare up at the sky. That was just the beginning for him. In 1961, he conducted the now infamous Milgram experiment. In this experiment, the participant was taken through a series of steps until they killed someone.

The participant was called the "teacher," and a confederate was called the "learner." Every time the learner made a mistake, the teacher was to give them one of a series of increasing electrical shocks. The meter had the word "lethal" at the 450-volt level. The learner was in another room, out of sight of the teacher.

Of course, the learner got a lot of the answers wrong, and the teacher kept giving them electrical shocks. The learner was begging them to stop. Every time the teacher didn't want to go on, the person playing the experimenter would say;

"Please continue" or

"The experiment requires that you continue" or

"It is absolutely essential that you continue" or

"You have no other choice; you must go on."

And, morbidly, 65 percent of them did continue—all the way to the end, even if the learner was no longer responding. A lot of the participants were angry, some were crying and hesitant, but 65 percent continued on to the end.

The ability to act independently had transferred from the participant (the teacher) to the man in the lab coat (the experimenter). This is called the "agentic shift," wherein a person carries out the orders of an authority figure without feeling responsible for their actions.

Notice that none of the instructions to continue were orders. In variations of the experiment, direct orders were not as effective. The oblique commands were the best.

Realize that agentic shift isn't always bad. When you take a doctor's prescription, you are giving over agency to another person. A whole genre of literature, the romance novel, involves a lot of giving over agency to another person.

It may not be fashionable to speak about dominance hierarchies, but they are everywhere—at home, work, the local PTA, and the corner bar. And the hierarchy shifts with the domain. A high-powered hospital CEO can go to the doctor and meekly submit to tests and prescriptions.

So what does this mean for the salesperson? You want to be or at least present as an authority in your domain.

The Utility of Authority

Obedience to authority is a powerful force to harness in a sales situation. As the author Chase Hughes says, "Authority is more influential than skill."

The projection of authority imbues everything you do. It has a halo effect; you can do no wrong, and everything you do is interpreted in a positive light. As a salesperson, you want what you are saying and doing to be interpreted in the best possible light.

There are many ways to project authority. The ones that have worked the best for me and are the easiest to implement are how you move, how you speak, and how you look.

How You Move

To quote Chase Hughes again, ".. head above your heart... head over your pelvis." In other words, stand up straight, just like your mom used to tell you. Also, "Never move faster than you could if you were underwater"—deliberately and a little slower than feels natural.

The people observing you will think of you as having authority based on the confidence they see in the deliberate movements of your body. The more fluid and natural you are, the more you will exude that leadership vibe.

How You Speak

Let me run you through a few points on how the way you speak influences the authority you wield.

- **Speak with purpose.** As we've established, what you say is valuable. Keep that in mind as you speak. If there is any doubt in your mind, it will show up in your speech.

- **Relax!** Sure, everything is on the line, but it always is. Utilize one of those thought-terminating clichés. "No matter the result, it is all going to be okay." Sink into that, believe it, and relax. Tension will change your voice, and you will come across as nonauthoritative. It will change how you move.

- **Establish trust.** Use the words and tempo of your customer to make them feel heard, safe, and at ease.

- **Speak slowly and deliberately.** Avoid filler words like "um," "ah," "like," and "you know." These will only detract from your credibility. When people get nervous, their rate of speech goes up; when they are confident and authoritative, the rate goes down.

- **Use pauses!** Emphasis builds tension around what you will say and gives the person a chance to think about the topic. Don't let what you say become one long run-on sentence.

At Halloween, one of the trick-or-treaters was a young girl. I gave her some candy. She stood there when everyone else was getting theirs, and she talked. One sentence ran into the other, and one topic ran into another.

It was cute for an eight-year-old, but don't be fooled—it is *not* cute from a professional trying to sell something.

- **Use a full and resonant voice.** Feel the vibration in your chest. Record yourself if you need some objective measures about what you are doing; in fact, record yourself as much as you can.

Recordings are objectively painful to listen to. I have dozens of recordings of myself that I never went back to—it was just too embarrassing. If you must, have someone else listen to them and give you suggestions. This is something you can swap with a co-worker, a trusted friend, or a coach. But you will get the most value if you listen to them yourself.

Be aware of the laws in your jurisdiction. It is always wise to get the permission of any other people besides yourself you are recording.

- **Get to the point.** Know what you want to say, and use the fewest number of words possible. Time is money.

- **Practice!** It doesn't matter what you know; it matters what you do. Put the reps in to make all of this natural and flow well, and you'll see the fruits of your labor in no time.

How You Look

What did Shakespeare say? "All the world's a stage, and all the men and women merely players." People expect you to fit their expectations. If you want to be an authority, it's simple: look like an authority.

When I did in-home presentations, I loved using a clipboard. It was a great symbol of authority as well as a practical writing surface. I didn't need to use a clipboard, of course, but I found that it really enhanced my image.

Even at the beginning of my fireplace career, I had my sales bag with tape measure, flashlights, and a form I co-created. These items, plus how I wielded them in my presentation, all added to my authority.

Be well-groomed, wear clean clothes, dress appropriately. These are things you'll have guessed on your own, but they're worth a mention.

Are you struggling to gain the respect of your customers? This might be the place to start. Remember that sales is very much a *fake it till you make it* situation; you can prepare, of course, but at some point, you need to take the leap, dress the part, and assume the role of the expert. You will look like you belong, and guess what? You do belong.

Making and Breaking Trances

How often do you catch yourself in autopilot mode? Maybe you walk into a room and forget why you're there, or you drive to work and realize you don't remember the last few miles. You were in a trance.

A trance is a state of mind in which your attention is focused on one thing, and everything else is blocked out. It's like when you watch a movie and get so involved in the story that you forget where you are. For a few hours, your mind is completely absorbed in what's happening on the screen.

We spend the majority of our lives in autopilot mode: going to work, going home, eating dinner, and going to bed. We do the same things over and over again without thinking about them. This is because our brains are hardwired to seek out patterns and conserve energy.

So what does this mean for you as a salesperson?

First, it's important to understand that trance is a natural state of mind. Your customers are going to be in a trance most of the time, and while it's possible to break that trance, it's difficult. Your best bet is to work with it.

Second, it's crucial to know how to make and break trances effectively. Making a trance means creating rapport with your customer, matching their language and body language, and using hypnotic language patterns to guide their thoughts and emotions. Breaking a trance means interrupting their habitual patterns, surprising them with something unexpected, and creating curiosity and interest.

Third, it's essential to know when to make and break trances. Making a trance is useful when you want to build trust, establish credibility, and influence your customer's subconscious mind. Breaking a trance is useful when you want to grab their attention, create urgency, and motivate them to take action.

One of the most powerful skills you can learn as a salesman is how to direct a customer's trance. A trance is a state of focused attention where the customer is more receptive to your suggestions and less critical of your claims. A trance can be induced by using language patterns, stories, metaphors, and other techniques that appeal to the customer's emotions and imagination.

Breaking a Customer's Trance

But before you can direct a customer's trance, you need to know how to break it. Why would you want to break a trance? Because sometimes the customer is already in a trance that is working against you. They might have a negative attitude toward salespeople, a preconceived notion about your product, or a resistance to change. In these cases, you need to break their trance and create a new one that is more favorable to your goals.

The only way to break a trance is to disrupt the pattern—to violate their expectations. When you do this, you interrupt their automatic thinking and force them to pay attention to you. You can use surprises, jokes, humor, or anything else that is unexpected and incongruent with their current trance. For example:

- If you're talking to a customer who has a poor perception of salespeople, you could try to break their trance by being honest and transparent. You could say something like, "I know you probably don't trust salespeople very much, and I don't blame you. There are a lot of dishonest people out there who just want to make a quick buck. But I'm not one of them. I'm here to help you find the best solution for your needs, even if it means recommending another product or service."

- If you're selling a product that is new to the customer, you could try to break their trance by creating curiosity and intrigue. You could say something like, "This product is unlike anything you've ever seen before. It has a feature that no other product in the market has. It's so amazing that I can't even tell you what it is right now. You have to see it for yourself."

But be careful not to overdo it. Disruption can be effective, but it can also be annoying or offensive if used too much or inappropriately. You don't want to shock or insult your customer; you want to surprise and delight them. You also don't want to disrupt their trance too often or too soon; you want to do it at the right moment and for the right reason.

The goal of disruption is not to destroy their trance but to transform it. Once you have their attention, you can then direct their trance in a more positive direction. You can do this by using rapport-building techniques, benefit-oriented language, storytelling, metaphors, and other trance-inducing methods. By doing this, you can create a new trance that is aligned with your goals and that makes the customer more likely to buy from you.

Keeping the Customer in Their Trance

What's the appeal of keeping someone in a trance?

Well, for one, it's much easier to get them to buy something as long as the path forward is clear and meets their expectations. When people are in a trance, they are more likely to make decisions based on emotion rather than reason. They are also less likely to question their decision.

In addition, when people are in a trance, they are more likely to trust authority figures. This is why salespeople use so many methods to get customers to focus on them. When someone is in a trance, they are less likely to be critical and more likely to take what the salesperson says at face value.

Your job is to not break the trance and to direct it in the direction you want. The easiest way to do this is by using language patterns. Language patterns are used primarily by hypnotists and neuro-linguistic programming practitioners. As a point of distinction: hypnosis is a method, and trance is a state. They are not the same.

Here are examples of my favorite three language patterns:

"**Can you imagine** the memories you will create with..."

"Considering your experience, **you probably already know** how effective sales skills can be."

"**If** you can feel the heat, **then** you realize how important having a fireplace is."

Language patterns are everywhere! Once you start to see and use them, your persuasion skills will go through the roof!

When you use language patterns in your sales pitch, you are assisting your customer in maintaining a trance. You are also providing them with a sense of certainty and security. This is why it's so important to be familiar with your product and the industry you're selling in. When you speak with authority about your product, it further helps to create a trance in your customer.

Language patterns also help to build rapport. When we use words that match our customer's values, beliefs, and desires, we create a connection with them. We show them that we understand them and that we have their best interests at heart. This makes them more likely to listen to us and follow our suggestions.

Keeping the customer in their trance is not about manipulating or tricking them into buying something they don't need or want. It's about helping them make the best decision for themselves by guiding them through a process that taps into their subconscious mind. It's about creating a win-win situation for both parties.

The next time you're selling something, try using some language patterns and see how they affect your results. You might be surprised by how much easier it is to keep the customer in their trance and close the sale.

Saying vs. Doing

One of the biggest challenges you'll face in making and breaking trances is convincing people to act. Let me explain why.

Remember that new hobby you wanted to start last year? You bought all the equipment, researched the best techniques, and even practiced a little bit. But then you never got around to actually doing it. Perhaps you know someone who talks about what they are going to do but never actually does it.

You've almost certainly experienced something similar in your own life. We all have grand plans and good intentions, but somehow they never quite translate into action. Why is that? And what does it have to do with trance?

The answer lies in the difference between saying and doing. When you say something, you are using language to express your thoughts and feelings. Language is a powerful tool that can help you communicate, persuade, and influence others.

When you do something, you are using your body and actions to create an effect in the world. Doing is more direct and concrete than saying. Doing also requires more energy and commitment than saying—you have to overcome inertia, resistance, and fear.

The problem is that most people confuse saying with doing. They think that by talking about something, they are actually doing it. They feel satisfied and accomplished by expressing their intentions without ever following through with action. This is a form of self-deception that prevents them from achieving their goals.

One of the best training sessions I ever went to was designed to help participants learn how to break this habit. The trainer had us complete the exercises before we even knew what they were. As we went along, he would explain the theory behind each task.

For example, one of the exercises was to walk around the block. We were told to do this before learning why it was important. Later the trainer explained that most people have a false sense of confidence in their physical abilities. They think they can walk further or faster than they actually can. By making us walk without knowing the distance, we were forced to pay attention to our bodies and their limitations.

The process of completing the task before learning the theory makes it much more effective. We weren't told what to do—we had to actually do it. This is a critical distinction. We also had experience that demonstrated the theory.

The same principle applies to trance work. If you want to help someone change their behavior or achieve their goals, you have to make them do something, not just say something. You have to guide them from imagination to action.

This doesn't mean that you should ignore language altogether. Language is still a useful tool for creating rapport, eliciting information, and suggesting possibilities. But language alone is not enough. You have to combine language with action.

One way to do this is to use what I call the "do-say" method. This is a simple technique that involves two steps:

1) Do: start by having your customer do something related to their goal or problem. It doesn't have to be big or complicated—just something that gets them moving and engaged.

2) Say: next, have your customer say something about what they did or how they felt while doing it. This helps them reflect on their experience and connect it with their language.

By mastering the art of making and breaking trances, you can become a more persuasive and effective salesperson. You can connect with your customers on a deeper level, understand their needs and desires better, and help them make the best decision for themselves.

Chapter Twelve

Cognitive Dissonance as a Sales Device

Back in the fifties, the social psychologist Leon Festinger heard about a doomsday cult called the Seekers, which believed that the world would be destroyed by a flood. The Seekers also believed that a spaceship was coming to take them away to safety before the end of the world. Festinger was intrigued and decided to study them.

Festinger joined the group, and what he found was fascinating. As the date for the spaceship's arrival drew nearer and nearer, the cult's members became more and more anxious. When the spaceship didn't show up, and there was no flood as predicted, members of the group became concerned that their beliefs and reality did not match.

Festinger's study showed that people are uncomfortable with the feeling of cognitive dissonance and will do anything to reduce it. In the case of the Seekers, they started to rationalize their beliefs. They told themselves that even if the spaceship didn't come, it was still a good thing because it meant that they were saved from the end of the world.

Then they picked a new date for the spaceship's arrival. And when that date came and went, they rationalized until they simply couldn't anymore. The Seekers disbanded and went their separate ways.

Festinger wrote his now-famous book, *When Prophecy Fails,* along with two colleagues and outlined his theory of cognitive dissonance. The theory states that people are uncomfortable with inconsistency and will do anything to reduce it.

There is one thing that your brain absolutely hates—pain. Your mind will do backflips to avoid pain. There are two ways it can do this: change your actions or change your beliefs.

In the case of cognitive dissonance, your brain will change your beliefs. This is because it's much easier to change a belief than it is to change an action. Of course, that's the second thing your brain hates—hard work—so your beliefs are on the chopping block first.

This is what we see in the Seekers cult. The members were willing to change their beliefs (and even rationalize them) in order to reduce the cognitive dissonance they were feeling.

Now, how can we bring this information into the world of sales?

Dissonance as a Sales Tactic

Cognitive dissonance is a powerful thing. It's what causes us to act impulsively, to make decisions based on emotion rather than reason. It's what makes us buy things we don't need and invest in schemes that are too good to be true.

When we're in the pain that is cognitive dissonance, we have to change either what we believe or the way we act. Out of the two, what we believe is the easier to change.

This is why it's so important for salespeople to be aware of cognitive dissonance. When we're able to create a sense of dissonance in the buyer's mind, we're much more likely to close the sale.

Let's look at an example. Imagine your customer is a husband whose wife has sent him in to talk about solar panels; however, the husband is skeptical. He's heard bad things about solar panels, and he's convinced that they're a complete waste of money.

This is where you come in with the hard-hitting facts. You can talk about the savings that solar panels can offer, you can talk about the environmental benefits, and you can even talk about the tax incentives. You can also come in with the emotions, such as the thrill of saving money, the pride of ownership, and how superior he will feel to his neighbors and friends when he brags about his new low bills.

The prospect wasn't aware of the facts before coming in, and he's left wrestling with the new information. Boom! You've set the stage for dissonance. The man's hard-held beliefs have been challenged, and he can no longer take them for granted. He's left with a choice: he can either change his beliefs or change his actions.

Most likely, he'll choose to change his beliefs. This is where you come in and offer him a solution. You can talk about the different types of solar panels available and make the installation process sound like a breeze.

The prospect is now in a much more receptive state. His brain is no longer working overtime to try and reduce the dissonance it's feeling; instead, he's thinking about the facts you've given him and the savings he's missing out on. He bites the bullet and signs for new panels.

This is the power of cognitive dissonance. It's what allows us to bypass reason and make decisions based on emotion. When we're able to create a sense of dissonance in the buyer's mind, we're more likely to close the sale.

Chapter Thirteen

Meaning-Making

I once took a class in the late nineties with an organization called The Forum which during the seventies was called EST (Erhard Seminar Training). It was held in a large, tightly packed room in San Francisco above the Burlington Coat Factory outlet store on Howard Street.

I didn't get a lot out of the experience, apart from one concept—humans are meaning-making machines. In simple terms, something happens, and then we decide what it means. That meaning-making can change the meaning of past events, too.

The meaning you create in a sales situation has the same effect. You can have an amazing sale, a beautiful execution, and then customer service ruins your progress one week later by giving them the wrong product. Suddenly, all the meaning you created around that sale is negated and changed; you're now the bastard who screwed up a customer's plans.

It's up to you what meaning you create around any particular event or interaction, and in your sales, you need to think carefully about the meanings you're creating for the customer.

Throughout my career, I learned that it was important to set realistic expectations for the customer. If there was ever an instance where I couldn't send the customer out the door with their product, I made sure to set realistic expectations for the next step.

Take construction, for example. There's no point in lying to the customer and saying that the job will be done in two weeks if you know realistically it will take four. They'll find out soon enough, and when they do, they're going to be pissed. All of the goodwill and the meaning you have created will turn negative. You might as well be honest and set expectations accordingly.

You may be hesitant to set any less-than-perfect expectations, but your customer knows that life isn't perfect. They're not looking for a fairy tale; they're looking for someone who can be upfront and honest with them, someone they can trust.

The Meaning of Owning an Item

There's another important aspect of meaning that we need to talk about, and that's the experience of owning an item. People purchase goods for a number of reasons: to make themselves feel better, to make a statement about who they are, and/or to project an image or idea.

When you're selling to someone, you need to be aware of what that purchase means to them. The Nike swoosh has come to represent athleticism and success, so when someone buys a pair of Nike's, they're buying into that image. The purchase becomes about more than just the functionality of the shoes.

Apple has taken this idea and run with it, creating an entire brand around the ideas of "premium" and "exclusive." When someone buys an iPhone, they're not just buying a phone; they're buying into the lifestyle and culture that Apple has created.

A thing is not just a thing; it exists as a signal in the human world. A fireplace can signal a commitment to the environment. An outdoor patio area can signal a person's wealth, communicating to the world that they've "made it."

If you can find out what a purchase means to your customer, you can better align your product with their needs. How do you do that? Ask questions about their values, then test the theories you come up with.

I always ask fact-based questions first: the where, when, how, etc., then I start to ask about their feelings and emotions. "It sounds like family is really important to you. What are some of your favorite things to do with the grandkids? What kind of family events do you like to host?"

This line of questioning leads to a better understanding of the customer. It allows you to start to see the world through their eyes. You can begin to understand what they're looking for in a purchase, and that's incredibly valuable information.

Let's say you're selling a product that doesn't quite fit into their worldview. You might be able to suggest a different product that does fit, or you might be able to help them redefine their values in order to make the purchase.

Either way, it's important that you understand the meaning your customer is attaching to the purchase. It's not sufficient to tack your own meaning onto the purchase and assume they'll buy into it. Understand that everyone attributes their own meanings to the things they buy, and that's something you need to account for in your sales process.

Levers of Control

There's another benefit that comes with taking the time to understand what a sale means to your customer; levers of control. Once you understand what a product or service represents to them, you can better influence their decision-making process.

For example, when selling a fireplace, it can mean many different things to the customer:

- It can represent the childhood they had and want to recreate for themselves or their children or grandchildren.

- It can represent the childhood wish they had and now want to create for themselves or others.

- It can represent security in case the power fails.

- It can represent pride in ownership.

Understanding the meaning the customer has around your product or service gives you a lever to move the customer in the direction you want them to go.

I walked into a store that sells water tanks. There's plenty of demand for these in drought-ridden Northern California, and I hadn't had much luck finding one; this store was my last hope. After browsing for a while, I found the perfect tank and approached the cashier.

"How much does this tank cost?" I asked.

"$1,500," he replied.

In response, I said, "Can you do a little better on that?"

This is a question I regularly felt thrown off guard by as a salesperson. When the salesperson began to appear flustered, it took me back to all the times I had been on the other side of that exchange. I realized that he was now at a disadvantage; he needed to sell me the tank, and I was in a position to negotiate.

If he'd known that my options were limited and that I was likely going to take the best deal he could offer, he would have had more control in the negotiation, but instead, he took the bait and gave me 7 percent off the price.

Embarrassingly for this salesman, I'd actually told him earlier that I'd done research and was running out of options. He could have controlled the negotiation better if he had remembered this information and used it to his advantage.

When you understand what a sale means to your customer, you can control the conversation more easily and get them to see things your way. You can also use this information to build a better relationship with your customer, one in which they feel like they're getting a good deal—and that's always a plus for any business.

This is what we call a lever of control: a tool you can use to get what you want in any negotiation. And believe it or not, salespeople have a lot more latitude than the people they are serving. Salespeople know the market, they have inventory, they can influence the timing of a delivery, they know the warranty, and they have extras they can provide.

Levers of control aren't just about negotiating price either; they can also pertain to the timing of a project, the delivery of a product, or anything else that's important to your customer.

The water tank salesman could have used his levers of control by simply asking me a few choice questions:

"Have you been looking at tanks for a while?"

"What's your budget?" or

"What are your options?"

And the answers would have given him a lot of information to work with.

Instead, he allowed me to take the lead in the conversation and missed out on an opportunity to make a full margin on a sale.

When it comes to meaning-making in sales, understanding what a sale means to your customer is one of the most important tools you can have in your arsenal. By using levers of control, you can get them to see things your way and make the sale a little easier.

Chapter Fourteen

Categories (or Where to Find the Money!)

For most people, their wants and needs are compartmentalized into different mental categories. You might have a mental category for things you need, such as food, clothing, and shelter. You also likely have categories for things you want but don't need, such as a new car or a vacation in Hawaii. Finally, you likely have a category of things you want and need, such as a new car that gets good gas mileage.

Your customers are likely to get locked into these categories, especially when a budget comes into play. If your product is in their "needs" category, the budget is going to have stretching room. If it's in their "wants" category, however, the budget is going to be a lot more rigid.

A key to getting people to buy your product is to switch it from their want category into their need category. When a customer says that there's "no room in the budget" for what you're selling, they're really saying "There's no room in this category." If you can get them to see your product as fitting into their need category, suddenly the budget has more room.

There are a lot of ways to switch categories, but let me show you how I used to do it for fireplaces.

The reality is that most people do not need a fireplace. They've got a heater that works just fine; they already have a decorative fireplace, or they may even have an outdoor firepit that suffices. The reason people buy fireplaces, therefore, is because they want one, so it doesn't fit into their need category.

However, what if I could convince the customer that a fireplace actually serves a function? Here's what I know about fireplaces:

- They are great to have as backup heating and lighting in the case of emergency outages.

- They can supplement the heating of a particularly cold room or area.

- They create a central gathering place in a room.

- They are perfect for atmosphere and ambiance.

The power outages option is incredibly easy to sell in Northern California; power companies are known to shut off power for hours at a time to avoid fires during the summer. The same can happen during the storm season. By explaining to the customer that a fireplace is a great investment for emergency situations, the product is instantly reframed in their mind as something they need.

Suddenly the not-so-flexible budget has some wiggle room.

The other way to switch categories is by playing up the benefits of what the product does. For example, if you're selling a weight-loss product, don't talk about the strawberry flavor or the cute packaging; talk about how much better the customer will feel after they've lost the weight. If you're selling a car, talk about how it will make their life easier by saving them time and energy.

Using Emotions to Switch Categories

Emotions are powerful forces; we've seen this a few times in past chapters, and the same applies in this one. When you can tap into your customer's emotions, they are more likely to be willing to make a purchase.

To go back to my fireplace example, I know that fireplaces tend to hold a lot of nostalgia and memory-based value for people. They remember cozy fires with their families, Christmas mornings with the fireplace blazing, and all sorts of other happy memories. I remember how my own living room would become the heart of my house in the winter, and how much I loved gathering around the fireplace with my friends.

By tapping into these emotions, I was able to get people to see their potential purchase in a different light. Suddenly the product wasn't just a want but a need that would fulfill an important function in their lives.

Your product will also have emotions associated with it, even if you don't realize it. I don't care if you're selling nail clippers or nuclear missiles—there are emotions at play.

If you're selling wheat flour, for example, you can talk up the warm scent of fresh bread that will fill the house on a winter morning. If you're selling a new phone, you can talk about how instantly they'll be able to connect with all their friends and family.

Find the emotions associated with your product, and then use them to convince the customer that they need it. Show them that working with you or using your product is the best way to fulfill their emotional needs.

Chapter Fifteen

Post-Close: Persuasion, Manipulation, and Inoculation

Çatalhöyük is the oldest known city as of this writing. It dates back to about 9,000 years ago. It was built because we like to live in groups, and it provided storage for food and protection from predators. Agriculture was invented about 12,500 years ago to create a more predictable and stable food supply. These two human inventions—agriculture and shelter—have allowed us to bring greater stability and predictability to our lives, and the human race has come to dominate the planet.

Peel your eyes off this page and look around you. Unless you are reading this book in the middle of a forest or desert, most of what you see around you was made by people: houses, furniture, cars, park benches, libraries—all created by human hands.

Just as we humans like to control and manipulate the physical environment, we also like to control and manipulate the social environment. In other words, to control and manipulate other people. This does not need to be malicious. Parents control and manipulate their children all the time to get them to bed on time or to go to school. Leaders manipulate their followers into following them. It is baked into our psychology.

Those are some of the more benign or beneficial forms of manipulation, but of course, there are more coercive variations. Occupying armies manipulate the masses so that they will not rise up. Abusive husbands manipulate their wives to stay with them despite their suffering.

I am well aware of the dark aspects of manipulation, and I would never suggest that these morbid instances are merely a natural outcome of our human tendencies. However, to manipulate simply means to handle or control something skillfully, so while there are perversions of this, there are also completely benign uses of manipulation—like sales.

This chapter is toward the end of the book for a reason. I think sales is one of the mildest forms of manipulation there is. I have read a fair number of books on so-called "dark psychology" or "covert manipulation techniques," and they all have this big disclaimer at the beginning, trying to get you to think the material in the book is "dangerous" and full of well-kept ancient secrets.

My book is not dangerous, nor does it contain any secrets (sorry to disappoint). You learned everything you needed to know in order to be a master manipulator by the time you were four or so. We all did. We also learned the consequences of manipulating people against their best interests.

By the time you are reading this book, you know what is right and what is wrong. You cannot really "talk" anyone into anything. You only give them enough excuses in order to justify their actions. Heck, an occupying army cannot control a country without the consent of the occupied. A few days after the occupation, people are going back to work, shops are open, and government offices are open for business. If the occupying army had to do all the work, the occupation would fail.

It's the same thing with sales. If you don't want to buy a widget, I can't sell you a widget. I can use all the techniques in this book, but if you feel like you don't need a widget, you won't buy one. However, if you think you might need a widget, I can take that "maybe" and turn it into a "must-have."

There had to be some desire there in the beginning. It's the same with love; if a potential partner is absolutely not interested, you are not going to interest them no matter what you do. It's the manipulation of their pre-existing notions that will land you the sale.

Making the Post-Close

One of the worst things in the world is to make a sale. The customer is happy; they're chortling to themselves as they leave your store or hang up your call. Perhaps they are a little anxious about the money they've just spent, but really, they are happy as clams.

But then—*then*—they go home and think about it. Maybe they do a little research on the internet. Maybe they talk to their brother-in-law or their crazy uncle, who happens to know everything about everything. All of a sudden, the sale gets shaky, and you find yourself handling an angry customer and a refund.

Salespeople hate it when this happens. And it can happen easily; they can bring the item back to the store, or they can dispute the charge on their credit card. If the sale took place in the home, they have a 72-hour cooling-off period here in the US. The sale can unravel for any number of reasons. That's why something called a "post-close" is vital to keep handy in your sales arsenal.

In martial arts, there's a concept called "Punching past the board." You'll have seen the videos of people chopping through wood with their bare hands; the trick is to look beyond the board. You don't just hit the surface. You push through the board and continue the strike even past the front plane.

It's an incredibly effective tactic, but it's all in the mindset. If your goal is to hit the front of the board, that's where your physical exertion will end; if you're focused on a point beyond the board, you unlock extra power and exertion that pulls your hand through even after it makes first contact.

A post-close works in much the same way—it's all in your mindset. Don't believe that the sale is over when your customer walks away smiling. Remind yourself that, in reality, the sale continues well after its close. You want to lock that sale down tight? Make it airtight and unassailable by preparing for the aftermath in advance.

Inoculation Theory

To explain how you can prepare for an effective post-close, I want to step back and discuss a phenomenon called "inoculation theory." Inoculation theory has been around since the early sixties, and you can find examples of politicians and preachers still using this technique. It's been validated many, many times over.

If you've ever been immunized against a particular virus or illness, you were likely given a small amount of the illness in order to build up your immunity. Inoculation is preparation—it is pre-exposing your body to a threat so when the threat itself appears, your body knows how to fight it.

Inoculation theory says that you should tell the customer what they can expect to hear from naysayers. This puts the customer on alert and arms them with a suitable rejoinder, "immunizing" them against potential threats to their satisfaction. It's similar to the levers of control in which you warn the customer that their construction project may experience delays; you prepare the customer for circumstances that may threaten their satisfaction after buying your product.

If I sell a customer a ticket to an upcoming stage production and I know that there have been mixed reviews about the play, it's in my best interests to tell them about it. It could even be presented in a joking manner. "I'm sure you'll love it, ma'am/sir, but be warned; some people might try to talk you out of it! That's just theater, though, isn't it?"

In doing so, I've simultaneously broken the tension and prepared them for potential naysayers. If a friend or relative talks trash about the play I've just sold them tickets to see, they'll have been prepared for that kind of response in advance and are less likely to get cold feet.

Let's dig a little deeper into this strategy because it's truly an essential one.

Inoculation Tactics

When using inoculation, there are two main avenues you can take: you can inoculate your customer against the message, or you can inoculate them against the messenger.

If you're familiar with their situation, inoculating them against the messenger could be pretty easy. Maybe they have that crazy uncle, or they have a brother-in-law who always assumes he knows better than everyone else. These are the messengers you can inoculate against.

You could say something like, "Oh, you know that crazy brother-in-law of yours? He always questions the things you do, doesn't he?" (See the double whammy there?)

When you get an affirmative, you might say, "Well, he's going to question this one too. And he's going to have some harebrained idea about why this is not the best item that you could possibly have. But you can just send him in to me, and I'll go through it with him."

Of course, you're not actually going to speak to the crazy brother-in-law. But now the customer has it in their mind that you know the value of this product more than anyone else and that you're confident you can set the record straight.

The other strategy is to inoculate your customers against the message. Your customers are going to be receiving messages about their purchase from all directions, especially now that we're all on the internet. The dreaded algorithm on their social media channels may still be throwing competitor products onto their news feed, claiming to have "Double the battery life!" or be "Half the price!" of the product you've sold them.

This is where you need to step in and shut down the messaging in advance. You might say something like this:

"People will point to anything on the internet these days and say, 'Look at this! It's so much cheaper!' But they don't realize our product is constructed from better material and it's made right here in the US. There's a strong company supporting it and a huge network of people available to service it should anything go wrong. But you know better, don't you?"

People want to be praised for their good sense; they don't want to be belittled. They don't want to think they've been taken advantage of, and they don't want to look like fools in front of their friends and family. This is why you should inoculate them against not only the people they speak to frequently but also the words those people are likely to use and the reasoning they are likely to give.

If someone says, "You could have bought that for less money on the internet!" you should have already prepared your customer with a backup. Perhaps there's a better warranty in store. Maybe you gave them an in-store exclusive add-on. Or, more simply, "You wouldn't have known which model to buy if you hadn't come to see me in-store!"

Remember, everybody's going to have buyer's remorse. Everybody's going to have second thoughts. Your goal is to allay those fears, giving them the armor they need to justify their purchase not only to themselves but to those around them.

Yes, we like to think of ourselves as free agents. *I do what I do because I want to do it! I bought this because I wanted to buy this!* But we're all beholden to somebody. And so when you make a sale, your customer not only has to justify these decisions to themselves; they're also going to have to justify these decisions to somebody else. Using a post-close will help with that.

Post-Close Pitfalls to Avoid

There's something that you need to be careful of with inoculation or post-close, and it has to do with making fun of the messenger.

If you have a crazy family member or friend, you're well aware of their quirks and their annoying tendencies. But you love them anyway. Not only that, but you'd also probably get defensive if someone tried to talk them down, even if what that someone is saying rings true.

This is why you need to be careful with inoculation. When warning your customer against potential messengers, it's crucial that you use a light tone. Don't go slamming their crazy brother-in-law as though you've got some sort of grudge against him. You need to discredit the bad messenger, but only subtly—just enough to plant the idea in your customer's mind.

"Don't listen to your stupid uncle!" isn't going to go down well.

"I know your uncle might have some different ideas, as he's very interested in this kind of product, but..." will give you a much better lead into discrediting him without stepping on any toes.

Another way that you can do this—and most of the time, you'll need to do this anyway—is to warn against no one in particular. You can almost guarantee that most people have a know-it-all friend or relative, so simply warn against this hypothetical person.

"I'm not sure who the camping geek is in your family, but I'm sure they'll have something to say about this tent..."

"I know you've probably got a tech fanatic or two in your life, and they are sure to have opinions..."

That way, you don't step on any toes at all because you didn't target anyone in particular.

Reactance Theory

Reactance is the anger or fear you may feel at the removal of some of your freedoms and the desire to get those freedoms back. If you combine inoculation with reactance theory, you can get an even stronger post-close.

These are emotions you do not want to invoke through your sales presentation. You want your customer to feel that their options are still open, even though you are leading them to reach a certain conclusion. However, there is another powerful way you can use this reactance theory, and that is to inoculate your customer.

Depending on the situation, you can warn your customer against other people who will try to make their decision for them.

"People will try to take away your freedom. They might try to force your hand." This sort of messaging prepares the customer for criticism by empowering them.

Another great line is, "You are your own person. You know your wants and needs better than anyone else!"

You need to be really careful with this because you can end up playing with fire. It's always best to keep things light and easy when making a sale, so invoking emotions of fear and anger can quickly turn sour for you. In certain circumstances, you may want to lock someone in and risk their emotional reaction.

It's going to be helpful in some situations, but I would use reactance with discretion. You'll be dealing with some very primal emotions, and fear is one of the most intense emotions you can deal with. So proceed at your own risk. Inoculation doesn't have to be hot and heavy.

Chapter Sixteen

A Sale Is Going to Be Made

Every time a salesperson and a prospect meet, a sale is going to be made. Either you will sell them on the necessity of your product or service, or they will sell you on the fact they do not need it. Even if they come to you with money in their pocket, ready to spend, there is always that last-minute hump to get over.

We have all heard the terms "sales" and "marketing" lumped together like they're a set of twins. But they are different. I define marketing as anything that draws a prospect to you. It might be an ad on Facebook, a TV commercial, or those rushed voices you hear over the radio. It could be a podcast or a blog that piques the prospect's interest.

Selling, on the other hand, is taking that prospect and turning them into a customer. You adapt your service or product to the prospect, or you adapt the prospect to your product or service.

Selling is one of those things that humans have been doing for a long time. It hasn't always been called sales; in fact, most of the selling you do is not called sales. Perhaps you have convinced someone at some point to fall in love with you, or you have convinced yourself to fall in love with someone else. You probably convinced a teacher that your classwork was good enough when it clearly wasn't. These are instances of selling, and all of us are engaged in the act.

Selling as a Human Habit

Humans love to modify their environment. We're too cold, so we kill an animal and use the skin as a blanket, or we take fibers from the environment and weave them into a nice coat. Water isn't consistently available? We build a dam, and the water backs up. Tired of being rained on? We build a house with a roof.

We humans modify our environments to suit us. It's the same with social environments.

What if you believe that capital punishment is immoral and that the government killing someone is just as immoral as one person killing another. But in your group, in your tribe, in your village, in your town, or in your nation, everybody else believes capital punishment is good and effective.

You are looked down upon for your aberrant belief. People shun you. Your family thinks you're nuts. You're the crazy uncle at Thanksgiving dinner. Nobody wants to engage with you, especially on this topic. This not only affects your family relationships, but it's difficult to get a job. It's difficult to get advancement in a job you already have, and you really have a hard time.

As a human, you've got a choice. You can either change your outward beliefs in order to fit in with everyone else, or you can remain true to your current beliefs and hope that you'll sell everyone else on your opinions one day. We often choose to conform and minimize our own rejection or discomfort. It's not necessarily a weak move to make; it's just part of our social habits.

If we go back to our capital punishment example, you may have said, "Oh, you know what? I don't believe in capital punishment. It's bad. It's immoral."

Then over the years, you get worn down, and you want to get promoted at work. Finally, you go, "All right, capital punishment. Just kill them. Just kill them all. Why should I care? Why should I suffer?"

As time goes by, something peculiar begins to happen. You convince yourself, "Oh, yeah, I've always been in favor of capital punishment." You start to edit your memories about this in order to cope with the cognitive dissonance it brings. Finally, you have been sold.

The other option then is to sell. If you have a child or when you were a child, you are familiar with this scenario. "Mom, Dad, please, can I? Pretty *please?* All my friends have these shoes. And they'll be so good for my sports, and they'll last forever!" This is an advanced selling technique where you align whatever it is that you're trying to sell with the goals of the other person. Isn't it crazy that most kids learn it straight-away?

So let's return to the capital punishment example for a moment—except this time, you are the one making the sale. You are determined to sell your neighbors and friends on the fact that capital punishment is wrong, immoral, and bad for society.

You could attempt to have a nice intellectual conversation. You could talk about how killing people is immoral and harmful and that it's no different from murder. But they'll rebut with their own logic. You need something more here.

So then, perhaps you make comparisons. What makes capital punishment any better than crimes of passion? And in fact, if you plan out a murder rather than committing it in a fit of rage, isn't that worse because you planned it?

You then appeal to the emotions. How is it fair to the family of the person being killed? They didn't do anything wrong. After the criminal is dead, they won't be receiving punishment anymore; their innocent family and friends will be.

They'll be dealing with debt, experiencing painful emotions, and facing public scrutiny—all of which they don't deserve.

See how quickly emotional appeal can swing an argument?

My entire point here is to demonstrate that making sales and being sold to is an occurrence we witness all the time in our day-to-day lives. It's not reserved for the car salesman at your local dealership.

As you are going through life, observe the ways that you adapt to your environment. How much are the people around you able to sell you on their beliefs and values? How much do you personally try to sell your own beliefs to friends and family in order to stabilize your environment?

You'll find that both selling and being sold take place fairly regularly. And that's not a bad thing. For example, why do we stop at a red light? Why didn't we all agree that green lights were what we stopped for? Or why do we drive on the right side of the road?

Maybe we're just being contrary to the British (and Australians and the South Africans), or the British are being contrary to us; I don't know. But either way, we drive on the right-hand side of the road. And that's one of the things that makes our civilization go so smoothly—when we all agree. Disagreement lies at the heart of some of the world's biggest problems.

What's the takeaway here? I want you to realize that sales isn't just a profession; it's everything. Gregor Mendel, the monk with the pea plants, had his theory of heredity sitting in a drawer for 100 years before it was rediscovered and sold to the public as scientific fact. The theory of plate tectonics—that the Earth's crust is floating on an ocean of magma causing earthquakes and volcanoes and other stuff like that—was widely derided for decades before it was sold as scientific knowledge.

The Self-Fulfilling Prophecy

Let's talk about self-fulfilling prophecies. Let's say you're a confident person. You're calm, cool, and collected, and able to make yourself look and sound successful. You are in a sales conversation with somebody who easily gets nervous around others. Their eyes dart from place to place, and it's obvious they aren't comfortable with you.

Noticing the way that your words affect their demeanor, you start to be a little more careful about the things you say and how you say them. This only makes the other person more nervous; you are mirroring their halted phrases and timid tone, which exacerbates the problem rather than reducing it.

Before you know it, you've had an incredibly uncomfortable conversation. You've definitely ruined the sale. This is what we call a self-fulfilling prophecy; you tell yourself the conversation is going poorly, and so that's exactly what happens.

We do this all the time, folks. A great example is in parenting. If you treat your child like a disobedient brat, never expecting anything good to come from their actions, it's difficult for that child to break out of the mold. If you tell yourself (and the child) that they are capable of surprising and positive things, you set the stage for much better behavior, attitudes, and self-esteem.

In sales, you need to remember that your customer is looking to you for cues. They are going to set their tone based on your mannerisms, and if you respond to their nervousness, anger, or boredom, they are going to increase that emotion twofold. Don't let the self-fulfilling prophecy thwart your sale!

Chapter Seventeen

Go Forth and Prosper

So there we have it—my sales advice, written out for your perusal (and maybe even adoption if you've found these lessons useful). I'm delighted that you've invested the time to read through my book. Hopefully, you've learned a few things you didn't know before you started. If nothing else, understand this: everything you need to be a successful salesperson is already within you.

One of my students is a sales engineer. Electrical systems are his specialty. He told me that once you understand the basic principles of electricity and electronics, you can create anything—it's all math and laying out the circuits.

Humans are not that simple, but the principles remain the same. When you learn the underlying principles of why we do what we do, then you can come up with novel and innovative solutions to your persuasive tasks.

That's all I've tried to do here: take a bunch of things you already know and have experienced in your day-to-day and apply them to sales. Why? Because I want you salespeople to understand that *everything is within your grasp.*

You don't need to spend thousands on guru-endorsed courses and glossy handbooks. You don't need to change who you are or practice your catwalk strut. If anything, you simply need to look at the skills you've already learned through the natural walk of life and then use them to your advantage.

If I can help you on that journey, reach out. Email me at <u>tony@tonynavarra.com</u> or check out my website at . I do monthly classes online, and I am available as a sales trainer or speaker for your organization.

Go forth and prosper.

Chapter Eighteen

Resources

A lot goes into the education of a salesperson. It seems we are a curious bunch and are always reading a book or article, listening to a podcast, or watching a video. It is all grist for the mill, and we know that somewhere, somehow, we are going to use this in making a sale.

Below is a list of books and podcasts that I have benefited from, and I think you will too.

Books

Influence: The Psychology of Persuasion by Robert Cialdini

The Challenger Sale: Taking Control of the Customer Conversation by Matthew Dixon and Brent Adamson

When Prophecy Fails: A Social and Psychological Study of a Modern Group That Predicted the Destruction of the World by Leon Festinger, Henry W. Riecken, and Stanley Schachter.

No Thanks, I'm Just Looking: Professional Retail Sales Techniques for Turning Shoppers into Buyers by Harry J. Friedman

Magic Words and Language Patterns: The Hypnotist's Essential Guide to Crafting Irresistible Suggestions by Karen Hand

Get People to Do What You Want: How to Use Body Language and Words for Maximum Effect by Gregory Hartley and Maryann Karinch

Thank You for Arguing: What Aristotle, Lincoln, and Homer Simpson Can Teach Us About the Art of Persuasion by Jay Heinrichs

The Ellipsis Manual: Analysis and Engineering of Human Behavior by Chase Hughes

Six-Minute X-Ray: Rapid Behavior Profiling by Chase Hughes

The Lost Art of Closing: Winning the Ten Commitments That Drive Sales by Anthony Iannarino

Cultish: The Language of Fanaticism by Amanda Montell

What Every Body is Saying: An Ex-FBI Agent's Guide to Speed-Reading People by Joe Navarro

Steal the Show: From Speeches to Job Interviews to Deal-Closing Pitches, How to Guarantee a Standing Ovation for All the Performances in Your Life by Michael Port

Find Out Anything from Anyone, Anytime: Secrets of Calculated Questioning from a Veteran Interrogator by James Pyle and Maryann Karinch

SPIN Selling by Neil Rackham

The Like Switch: An Ex-FBI Agent's Guide to Influencing, Attracting, and Winning People Over by Jack Schafer

The Science of Storytelling: Why Stories Make Us Human and How to Tell Them Better by Will Storr

Podcasts

Huberman Lab Dr Andrew Huberman

Opinion Science Andy Luttrell

The Jordan Harbinger Show Jordan Harbinger

You Are Not So Smart David McRaney

About the Author

Tony Navarra is a salesman, speaker, and author who has a passion for helping people achieve their goals. He has over twenty years of experience in various sales roles, from selling patio furniture at street fairs to closing deals with high-end clients in their homes. He has also studied the psychology of persuasion and influence and has applied his knowledge to his own sales career and to teaching others how to sell more effectively.

In his book, *Killer Sales Solutions: 12 Knock 'em Dead Ways to Prepare, Present, and Close the Sale*, Tony shares his hard-won knowledge for becoming a sales superstar. He reveals how to use your natural curiosity, exuberance, and enthusiasm to connect with prospects, overcome objections, and close sales faster. He also shows you how to adapt your sales style to different situations and personalities and how to use storytelling, humor, and emotion to persuade and influence.

Tony Navarra is not just a sales trainer. He delivers his message with energy, humor, and enthusiasm that will keep you engaged and entertained. He will inspire you to take action and achieve your sales goals.

Contact Tony at tony@tonynavarra.com